# Sarah's
## *Journey of Faith*

### Volume 2:

*From Water to Fire*
*The Prison Years*

Selected Passages Primarily from the Book of Acts

*Sarah Liu*

WESTBOW
PRESS®
A DIVISION OF THOMAS NELSON
& ZONDERVAN

WestBow Press books may be ordered through
booksellers or by contacting:

WestBow Press
A Division of Thomas Nelson & Zondervan
1663 Liberty Drive
Bloomington, IN 47403
www.westbowpress.com
1 (866) 928-1240

ISBN: 978-1-4908-8645-9 (sc)
ISBN: 978-1-4908-8646-6 (hc)
ISBN: 978-1-4908-8644-2 (e)

Library of Congress Control Number: 2015910083

Print information available on the last page.

WestBow Press rev. date: 07/27/2015

# Contents

*To my mom*

# Foreword

Volume 1 of *Sarah's Journey of Faith* was dedicated to the early years up to her conversion. Volume 2 is specifically about Sarah's spiritually formative years from her baptism in water to her baptism in fire.

John the Baptist said, "I baptize you with water. But one who is more powerful than I will come, the straps of whose sandals I am not worthy to untie. He will baptize you with the Holy Spirit and fire" (Luke 3:16).

Some may remark that Volume 1 was culturally fascinating and intriguing, but Volume 2 is a turbulent journey of faith, as she never knew what was around the next corner. Some may think that they could never survive such turbulence. Well, neither did Sarah. She is quite clear on this point. Only Jesus Christ can give the strength to endure, survive, and be victorious. The apostle Paul said, "I can do all this through him who gives me strength" (Phil. 4:13).

Do not underestimate what Christ can do through you. I trust that this devotional will encourage and embolden you. Have a blessed journey of faith.

E Perez Romero
Pastor, Professor of Philosophy, and Religious Rights Activist
exodus8one

# Acknowledgments

I will take this opportunity to acknowledge my mom at length and to thank her for her life and influence. To me, this is only one episode of her loving life.

As you will read, my father and brothers provided fierce opposition to my mother and me. As a result of us being followers of Jesus and my father ("Your Jesus or me!") giving us an ultimatum, we were forced out of our house for choosing Jesus. In anger, my father and brothers gathered all our belongings and sleep clothes and tossed them out of the house and onto the street. There we two stood in the cold winter day, slowly regaining our composure and carefully picking up our belongings.

I asked my mom, "What do we do now?"

She replied, "Even if we have to beg, we will still believe in Jesus. Let's gather everything and go."

So definite was her resolve that I took courage in her determination. I look back now and see clearly that without her example I would not have survived such harsh opposition. I thank God for giving such a mom to me.

Once we put our belongings on our backs, we walked about aimlessly. We came to a group of community workers digging ditches for village improvements. When they saw us, they laughed and jeered at us, having heard the rumor that we chose Jesus over our family. I was at once ashamed at being the object of scorn and also at peace, reminding myself of the humiliation of my Jesus.

After passing the jeering crowd, I asked Mom, "Where are we going?"

She related a church song that described the story of the rich man and Lazarus (Luke 16:19-31). The song lyrics reminded us that Lazarus had nothing—not even a place to be buried—but he loved God, and heaven awaited him. Even though we were without home or family, God was in our hearts, and we had heaven waiting for us too.

After a long, aimless walk down the path—alone with our thoughts, exhausted, hungry, and cold—we stopped to unburden ourselves from our belongings. As nightfall approached, Mom and I bowed before the Lord and cried out to Him for help. We sensed His peace, but we were still uncertain about what to do next.

Not long after our prayer, a sister from the church was pedaling a bicycle past us. All of a sudden, she recognized my mom from church meetings and inquired, "Why are you here?"

Mom explained the events from earlier that day, and the sister insisted that we come home with her.

When we arrived at her home, the sister's husband and two children welcomed us. That night, after eating a hearty dinner and feeling exhausted from the day's ordeal, I went to bed and prayed myself to sleep. My mom stayed up to speak with our sister in the Lord.

Early the next day, the sister called my relatives and explained our plight to them, and my auntie insisted we come and stay with them. We gathered our belongings and waited for Auntie to come collect us. We thanked our dear sister for rescuing us from the night and giving us food and shelter. Then we were off to Auntie's.

After a week at Auntie's, she negotiated with my father and brothers about allowing us to return and said it was shameful for them to treat us that way. They eventually relented and permitted our return under the following conditions: We must choose between Jesus or the family, and if we choose our family, then all would be well. If not, then we must live in segregation.

This was not "separate but equal." Instead, mom and I were relegated to a small room within our detached kitchen. To make matters worse, they also separated the land parcel that the state issued for us to work and grow our own produce.

My mom was used to this kind of hard work, but it was foreign to me. As the youngest, my daddy and brothers spoiled me. I never had to work the field.

I never needed to learn. Now for the very first time, Mom and I were left to ourselves to work for our food, and the family would not lift a finger to help.

Again turning to Mom, I cried, "How can we do this? I know nothing about farming!"

Mom replied in the most assuring tone, "With the Lord's help I will teach you how to plant, grow and harvest the field."

We put our backs and hands to work—aches, blisters, and all. Yet as we surveyed the community parcels, we noticed that all wheat crops from the other parcels were tall and green and ours were comparatively meager and yellow. Nevertheless, we would go to our little room with peace and joy in our hearts.

Mom decided that we needed to fertilize our field.

"How do we do that?" I asked. "We have no money for fertilizer!"

"Here's what we will do" she said, "After our morning prayer and Bible reading we will go throughout the village and collect animal dung."

So we set off to do just that every morning. I collected the chicken dung; my dear mother managed the cow dung. At the end of the day, we would bring our dung treasure back to our field and evenly distribute it.

As the Lord would have it, I never saw the harvest of our crops. Our dear relative received notice from the church that they would begin a discipleship school, and he raced to our field to tell us of this new development. Upon receiving this news, my mom insisted I go to this school and said she would continue with the field. She was far more enthusiastic about the discipleship school than I was. (In Volume 1, I related the story of my parents' inability to send me to high school, let alone college.)

In her sincere and genuine happiness for me, she exclaimed, "Now you can go to Heaven College!"

I could see her overwhelming joy in finally sending me to my higher education.

This was one of the last occasions when I was with my mom. After she harvested the crops, she baked her special bread with the wheat and personally transported it to our Bible school. Upon delivery, she chose not to disturb me in my studies and quietly slipped away without meeting with me. In her heart, she didn't want to meet, lest I got homesick and abandoned my Heaven College.

Though we were apart, my mom has always been close to my heart. After my escape from China and arrival in the safety of the United States, she is still in my heart.

Mom went home to the Lord in 2013. She has entered the gates of Heaven College for all eternity.

# Part 1

# Called to Be an Evangelist

# After My Conversion

Those who accepted his message were baptized,
and about three thousand were added
to their number that day.

—Acts 2:41

---

After my three days of hearing the gospel and surrendering to Christ, I continued an additional day at my auntie's house while eagerly reading the Bible and copying verses. My mother hurried home, knowing trouble would await me, and she tried to smooth the way.

The next day, I walked all the way home while rejoicing and singing songs to the Lord. I had no thought about what was about to happen. As I approached my home, from afar, I saw my father and brothers at the gate. As I got closer, I saw anger in their faces, but I was not alarmed.

My father insisted that I sit in a chair that had been prepared, unbeknownst to me, for my questioning and angrily asked, "Where have you been these last three days?"

"I have come to believe in Jesus!" I said.

At that moment, my father, with my brothers' consent, slapped me across my face with such force as to eject me from the chair. So unexpected was this response to the beautiful thing that God had done. Yes, I was added to their number, but I was on immediate notice that the cost would be steep.

# What Do You Think?

Can you recall the early days of your salvation and how you felt when you were opposed? How did Jesus comfort you?

Today's Reflection

_____

_____

_____

_____

_____

_____

_____

_____

_____

_____

_____

_____

_____

_____

_____

_____

Today's Prayer

_____

_____

_____

_____

Day 2

# A Voice in the Mountains

All the believers were together and
had everything in common.

—Acts 2:44

———————

Heaven College (seminary) was open to those who
desired to be involved in ministry, especially as
an evangelist. It all began with a four-day prayer
meeting where 30 to 35 young people came together
for intense prayer and teaching on discovering God's
purpose and understanding our worth in the Lord.
At the conclusion of the four days, our teachers
interviewed us to determine if being evangelists
would be right for us.

Once admitted into seminary, we were sent to
a mountain region, where a large house was made
available for our use. This was our daily schedule:

| | |
|---|---|
| 5:30 a.m. | Rise and shine |
| 6:00 a.m. | Bible reading |
| 6:30 a.m. | Prayer |
| 8:30 a.m. | Breakfast |
| 9:30 a.m. | Bible class |
| 1:30 p.m. | Break time |
| 2:00 p.m. | Bible class |

| 5:30 p.m. | Dinner |
| 6:30 p.m. | Homework |
| 9:00 p.m. | Prayer |
| 10:00 p.m. | Bedtime |

One early morning during our prayer time, we heard the alarm from our watchman that meant police were coming. We were instructed to make way for our teachers to escape and then pick up our Bibles and run to our prearranged rendezvous point.

In our escape up the mountain, we were met by a gentle rain and cold temperatures. When we met up with our leaders, they had plastic tarps that we huddled under. Arm in arm and side by side we sat, praising God for our escape. At night, our leaders stood watch over us as we tightly huddled together to stay warm and get some sleep.

The next day, we heard a woman singing in the distance.

*Who could that be?* was our collective thought.

The lyrics were becoming clear. It was a church song that said, "Jesus is looking for His one lost sheep." We knew that someone was searching for us.

"It's our cook!" we all exclaimed.

She came with a large bundle of prepared food— rice and cucumbers—for us! But she only had six bowls and six sets of chopsticks. We all stared at each other, and none dared to be the first. Our leaders took charge and commanded people to eat as they pointed us out.

We felt very close to each other, dearer than family. We had our very first brush with danger, and we beheld the great love and sacrifice of our leaders and precious cook. At this moment, emotion came over us, and we cried tears of thanksgiving for the Lord's care and His faithful servants. This was my first profound experience of "all the believers were together."

# What Do You Think?

How hard is it for you to surrender your possessions
even when the cause is good or loving?

Today's Reflection

_____
_____
_____
_____
_____
_____
_____
_____
_____
_____
_____
_____
_____
_____
_____
_____
_____

Today's Prayer

_____
_____
_____
_____
_____

Day 3

# Sent Out and Saying Good-Bye

> While they were worshiping the Lord
> and fasting, the Holy Spirit said, "Set
> apart for me Barnabas and Saul for
> the work to which I have called them."
> —Acts 13:2

After escaping three police raids and relocating our seminary four times, we learned not only the Bible but ways to be prepared for flight and hardship. We were a very close class of twenty-four evangelists.

Now the day of graduation had come. Because we were the first graduating class and ceremonies were still evolving, our commencement was very simple: prayer and commissioning. That night, excitement of what was to come filled us all. The teachers and elders came together and after much prayer and discussion with each graduate, we were all assigned to a particular geographical area of ministry. We packed our simple belongings. All the girls got their hair cut short for easy management, and we exchanged the little clothing that we had with each other. One would give a blouse; another would offer this or that small item. We just wanted to share with one another, knowing it would be a long time until we saw each other again.

Unable to sleep, I tossed and turned in great expectation of the holy adventure set before me. Early the next morning, while it was still dark, we prayed for each other, cried together, and promised to remember each other daily in prayer as we said our good-byes.

With our backpacks ready, Bibles in one hand, and ten yuan (Chinese currency equaling about one US dollar) in the other (our allotment for three months), we started off to the local bus station.

So profound was the sense of being set apart for the work of the Lord that my heart was racing within me as my coworker and I boarded the bus for our holy destination. How sweet and precious to me are those defining moments. He is faithful.

# What Do You Think?

Can you recall a moment in time, other than your conversion, when you were aware that this moment was special?

Today's Reflection

_____

_____

_____

_____

_____

_____

_____

_____

_____

_____

_____

_____

_____

_____

_____

_____

_____

Today's Prayer

_____

_____

_____

_____

# Part 2

# Baptism in Water

Day 4

# Washing My Sins Away

Peter replied, "Repent and be baptized,
every one of you, in the name of Jesus Christ
for the forgiveness of your sins. And you
will receive the gift of the Holy Spirit."

—Acts 2:38

---

Because of persecution, our church baptized only once a year. In fact, I had never witnessed a baptism myself. But it was my time to walk in obedience of the Lord.

This was not a celebrated public display. Instead, it was a quiet church event conducted in the dead of winter during the early morning hours (just after midnight). We gathered far away from the public view and even farther from city police and officials. We would gather at homes prior to our trek to the local river. Then in the early morning hours, we would quietly make our way to our designated site.

Our leaders directed us to sit in rows and call upon the Lord. There, I bowed facedown in prayer and silently waited my time for baptism. Finally, I was tapped to go into the freezing waters. I removed my heavy winter jacket and only presented myself with my baptismal gown. I was not focusing on the fact that the waters were cold or it was night. Rather, my attention at the moment was one of curiosity. *What will they do to me? What will happen next?* I thought.

One of the two brothers extended his hand to me, and I positioned myself between them.

One asked, "Are you Sarah Liu?"

I replied, "Yes."

They then asked, "Are you dead to the world?"

"Yes."

Their final question was, "Will you be buried with Christ and rise again in newness of life?"

"Yes!" I answered resoundingly.

At that point, they invoked the ancient baptismal formula of Father, Son, and Holy Spirit.

The last words I heard before I went down into the water were, "Wash away your sins!"

A brother led my back to the bank. Despite the harsh conditions, my heart was full of light on that dark night and bursting with joy in that cold evening.

After making our way quietly back to the village, we dried off and prepared for bed. I lay down that night and reviewed the evening's activities. It was as if I were born again ... again.

# What Do You Think?

Have you walked in obedience to the Lord, following Him in waters of baptism? If not, don't hesitate to do the right thing. If you have obeyed, then rejoice that you are learning the beginning steps of obedience.

Today's Reflection

_____

_____

_____

_____

_____

_____

_____

_____

_____

_____

_____

_____

_____

_____

_____

_____

Today's Prayer

_____

_____

_____

_____

_____

# Part 3

# Baptism in Fire

Day 5

# Forewarned and Forearmed in the Spirit

"We must go through many hardships to
enter the kingdom of God," they said.

—Acts 14:22b

---

"Whoever wants to be my disciple must deny
themselves and take up their cross daily and follow
me" (Luke 9:23) was our evangelist's constant
reminder. In the early days of my conversion, this
verse was a relentless theme. For us new believers, it
was common knowledge that something bad would
happen to us if we chose to live for Jesus.

Having the certainty of hardships ahead helped
us brace for what was to come. No one was taken
by surprise when trouble actually came upon us. The
terror effect was diminished but not eliminated. To
be told that hardships were coming helped. To see a
sister or brother arrested was always of grave concern
but accepted because no other earthly recourse was
available to us in either court or society. But being
arrested, as you will learn, has its own set of fears
to overcome.

In those early days, I made up my mind that I
wanted to carry the cross like Jesus did. Even though

it would be hard, I nevertheless desired to walk as He did. There was no doubt about following Jesus to the ends of the earth. The evangelist would also remind us that, wherever the preaching of the Gospel would take us, He would be there.

Hardship, yes. His presence, yes and amen!

# What Do You Think?

Have you ever known danger or hardship, and have you invited Jesus to be with you in it? What was your greatest hardship, and how did He deliver you from it?

Today's Reflection

_____

_____

_____

_____

_____

_____

_____

_____

_____

_____

_____

_____

_____

_____

_____

Today's Prayer

_____

_____

_____

_____

Day 6

# A Witness to Injustice

So they stirred up the people and the elders and
the teachers of the law. They seized Stephen
and brought him before the Sanhedrin.

—Acts 6:12

*Who will be first?* was in the back of my mind. But to
my surprise, it was a key helper and brother named
Baijun Li, a person who, by all appearances, could
least afford being arrested. Brother Li was the most
dependable brother in our work. Besides having his
own immediate family, he also had his special needs
brother and widow mother living under his care.

His home was our primary base of operation in
that region, and he and his wife were exceedingly
generous to our work in many ways. We could always
depend on him to be our biggest supporter.

As we ministered the gospel in his village one
day, we heard rumors that the Public Security Bureau
(PSB) was cracking down on Christians and their
sympathizers. It was recommended that we move
to another location, one where neither we nor our
supporters would be caught. That night, we stayed at
the home of sympathizers (non-Christian) and were
out of harm's way.

The next day, Baijun's wife hurriedly came to us and, with distress on her face said, "My husband has been arrested! It is not safe for you to be here." "How was he arrested?" we enquired. She replied, "The police laid in wait for my husband to return home, and then, they violently broke into our home and dragged him away to the police station. You must flee this place or they will come after you next." We heeded her counsel and departed. She was distraught, yet she had her wits about her to warn us that the crackdown had now come here.

Witnessing this episode only emboldened us to preach more fervently and passionately until our time of hardship should come.

# What Do You Think?

What do you feel when friends like Baijun are treated unjustly? Does your anger lead to vengeance, or does it deepen your resolve and faith?

Today's Reflection

_____
_____
_____
_____
_____
_____
_____
_____
_____
_____
_____
_____
_____
_____
_____
_____

Today's Prayer

_____
_____
_____
_____
_____

# First Arrest and Jail

# In the Attic

But his followers took him by night and lowered
him in a basket through an opening in the wall.

—Acts 9.25

---

*The crackdown has begun!* I thought. *We must move
to another location. This is no longer safe.*

When night fell, my coworker and I stealthily made
our way to another village where the crackdown had
not spread ... or so we thought. When we arrived at
our destination, the rain was pouring down steadily,
and I thought that was good for us. With fewer people
on the streets and us remaining in the dark of night,
we would be much safer to move about. These were
some of the lessons we learned in seminary, ways to
move about stealthily.

Unbeknownst to me, an informant, who identified
us as Christian from another village, spotted my
coworker and me. Because he was the village
manager, he felt it was his duty to report us to local
police as troublemakers.

When we arrived safely (so we thought) to our
member's home, we changed our rain-soaked clothes
for nice, dry clothes. We were invited immediately

for snacks before the dinnertime. We were happily sharing the day's events and enjoying our snacks.

A word about Brother Xu, at whose home we were staying. His craft was carpentry, and he remodeled his attic as a hideaway for visiting Christians like us. When we arrived, he quickly put our things in this sanctuary for safekeeping and in anticipation of any police raid.

As we were excitedly talking about the day's events, we heard noises outside a nearby window. I studied the view, but because of the translucent nature of the glass, I could not see out, and they could not tell what was inside. However, above the window was a long, narrow panel with clear glass.

I saw a person spying on us, and he saw me. My coworker and I jumped out of our seats and ran upstairs to the attic. We heard people pounding on the windows and kicking in doors. The family below was frantic. Brother Xu delayed opening the door until he knew we were safely in the attic. Unfortunately in our scramble into the attic, I knocked over the stack of boxes that we climbed to reach the attic door, and they came crashing down with a loud thump!

Brother Xu's wife signaled that we were in, and their little boy, upset by all the calamity, was crying loudly. Finally, the police broke through and asked them to turn over the troublemakers. Brother Xu was harshly treated with beatings, and his wife was abused. Brother Xu told them that we had already left and were no longer in the home.

"You lie!" was the lead officer's hostile response.

He then ordered for his fellow officers to thoroughly search the home. A systematic search was conducted, and we were not found. My heart was racing and about ready to pound out of my chest, but we made not a sound. We heard one of the officers report that the search was complete. The lead officer rejected that conclusion and told them to search again.

He then turned to Brother Xu and said it was impossible for us to escape unnoticed. The entire village had surrounded the house, armed with flashlights, and they saw no one leave!

We later found out, after our release from jail and reunion with the family, that the villagers were told that we had supernatural powers and could fly away in the night to avoid capture and arrest. Many were there to see if we could fly. There was no chance of that.

Just when we thought we were clear, the relentless lead officer insisted that we were still in the house. Then another officer said that, just before the front door was broken down, they heard a loud crash on the second floor. Another very intensive search was conducted, but they poked and prodded everything this time, and we were found.

What a rollercoaster of emotions! Once they uncovered our hideaway, I was resolved that we would be arrested, so I went quietly with no fight and no screaming. *Lord, a basket through the opening of a wall would be nice*, I thought.

# What Do You Think?

Can you recall the last time you were trapped with nowhere to run? Since the Lord knows our every situation, have you experienced the liberation of acknowledging Him in the midst of the situation?

Today's Reflection

_____
_____
_____
_____
_____
_____
_____
_____
_____
_____
_____
_____
_____
_____
_____
_____

Today's Prayer

_____
_____
_____
_____
_____

Day 8

# At the Police Station

But when they did not find them, they dragged
Jason and some other believers before the city
officials, shouting: "These men who have caused
trouble all over the world have now come here,
and Jason has welcomed them into his house."
—Acts 17:6-7

---

So here we were, criminals of the state. We were
physically dragged out of Brother Xu's home and
pushed, kicked, knocked down, and punched all the
way to the car. I thank the Lord I had no fear for my
personal well-being, but concern about Brother Xu
and his family consumed me. Because of us, danger
had befallen them, yet I also was aware, especially
telling were the look on their faces as we were
dragged away. It was as though they were deeply
sorry that they had not protected us as they should.
This is God's love. We were afraid for them, and they
were doing all in their power to prevent our being
taken in.

We saw police beating down Brother Xu as we
were hurried away to the police station. Adding to
our grief was the fact that they would have to face

village humiliation because of us for who knew how long?

I thought to myself, *Because Brother Xu was a brand-new believer, this experience could work against him and discourage him out of the faith.*

En route to the police station, my coworker and I were handcuffed to each other in the backseat of the police car. We were trained in seminary that, if we were caught, we were to follow the example set by Jesus when He was questioned. He spoke not a word to His interrogators.

Though we were forbidden to speak to each other, we spoke volumes with our eyes and knew we had to put our lessons into practice. We were not afraid of what would happen to us. We just keep Jesus before us as our Lord and our example.

Upon arrival, my coworker and I were separated, and I was taken into what appeared to be a lunchroom, where I was handcuffed to a bench. The cuffs were hurting my wrists, but this was no concern to them. By the time I was handcuffed to the bench, it was about seven in the evening. I was interrogated on and off until midnight.

First, they asked for my name. With my head bowed, I offered no answer.

Grabbing my hair, he yelled, "Your name! Tell me your name!"

Again, I gave no answer.

This enraged him further, so he began kicking me. He grabbed my ears and pulled my head about, screaming, "Don't you hear me?"

Still, I gave him no answer. And so it went the entire night.

Sometimes, he would appeal to me, "You are so young. Your future is ahead of you. You should be studying in college." Then he pulled the shame card, "You should be at home caring for your parents, but look at you, abandoning your family duties. And for what?"

After threats, appeals, increased violence and threats, and more commonsense appeals, I still gave no answer.

So convinced were the police that we were troublemakers that they were totally blind to the truth and glory of Jesus. They could only see their narrow ideology and could not comprehend beyond that. *Surely*, thought I, *a veil was placed over their hearts and minds.*

Two weeks later, while in jail, I received a gift from Brother Xu, "Five yuan!" I shrieked.

The five yuan was only a symbol that the Lord strengthened them and what I feared did not happen, but they grew in love and faith in the Lord Jesus Christ.

Brother Xu and his family paid a high price for receiving and protecting us. I think that, like Jason, Brother Xu was abused by the world but esteemed by God. Thank you, Lord, for the Jasons and Brother Xus of the world.

# What Do You Think?

Who has the Lord used to rescue or protect you in your life? Why not give thanks to the Lord for them at this moment of reflection?

Today's Reflection

_____
_____
_____
_____
_____
_____
_____
_____
_____
_____
_____
_____
_____
_____
_____
_____
_____

Today's Prayer

_____
_____
_____
_____
_____

Day 9

# When the Door Closed behind Me

About midnight Paul and Silas were praying
and singing hymns to God, and the other
prisoners were listening to them.

—Acts 16:25

---

When the cell door closed behind us, we heard, "Are you newcomers?"

"What?" we replied.

"Are you newcomers?" the other women in the cell asked.

"Yes," we answered.

Then they turned to the jailer and asked him, "What's their crime?"

He answered, "Go back to sleep."

A word about the jail arrangements for women. Usually, one cell is set apart for women, as was the case in this one, *Sha Yang* (The Mouth of the Tiger). And the one cell had a hierarchical order, usually established by seniority and jailhouse toughness. As newcomers, we did all the dirty jobs the others refused to do. For the Lord's sake, we gladly took our place in the hierarchy as the last and least of a cell of ten women.

As we looked about us, I couldn't believe my eyes! "Sister Zi Shou!" I exclaimed in delight and saw a familiar face and a warm smile. I was rejoicing in the Lord, not because Sister Zi Shou was in jail but because we had the company of another sister, senior to us.

Strangely that night, as we all took our sleeping places on the floor, we three sisters kept warm by slumbering huddled together. We experienced joy in the midst of difficult and dark times.

The most senior of the inmates, as was the case with all the others in the cell, were in jail charged with either prostitution or drug possession. Because we were so different from them, they asked, "Why did you come here?"

We replied, "We believe in Jesus!"

As you can imagine, unbelievable boredom marks jail life. As part of our initiation rite, we were put through a gauntlet of hostility to which the Lord allowed us to endure and overcome. Afterward we took great comfort in singing to the Lord. Our fellow inmates didn't shush us. Rather, our unflappable joy amused them.

On several occasions, the senior inmate would announce to the others that it was time for Christians to sing. And sing we did! Her invitation to carol was not a request but a demand as if it were part of the daily schedule and now it was time for us to do our part. So we gladly did our portion, hoping the words of the songs would find their way to their hearts.

For the next two weeks, we settled into our jailhouse routine until I was separated from the other sisters and sent to county jail near my hometown. I completed my sentence, and I was released. (Sentencing is arbitrary.) I was given several opportunities to share my faith, and the songs of joy never departed my heart.

# What Do You Think?

The Apostle Paul's experience was earthshaking and extremely dramatic. Do you think you can survive circumstances of deprivation? Just you and Jesus, together through the difficulty?

Today's Reflection

_____

_____

_____

_____

_____

_____

_____

_____

_____

_____

_____

_____

_____

_____

_____

_____

Today's Prayer

_____

_____

_____

_____

_____

Day 10

# Pressured by My Family

From now on there will be five in one
family divided against each other, three
against two and two against three.

—Luke 12:52

---

Since I left *Sha Yang*, I had grown accustomed to my new surroundings. It was so much better than the last confinement. After about three weeks and approximately two to three times a week, I would be abruptly taken from my cell at all hours for interrogation.

As interrogations go, they would appeal to me through kindness and concern once, then the next time would be with hostility and intimidation. No matter what environment they created, I knew I was never alone and would never deny my Lord Jesus.

This frustrated them to no end. They would constantly implore me to call on my family to visit and to provide extra money to make jail life more comfortable. The Spirit gave me enough wisdom to see through their strategy.

Of all temptations I would face, my family was the most powerful. After the jail officials failed to get my consent to bring in my family for a visit, they took the initiative and manipulated my family to come visit me and talk me out of this religious superstition against the state.

One afternoon, I was called out. Thinking it was going to be another round of interrogation, I was surprised that I was led to the visitors' area. There, my uncle (my mom's younger brother), my brother, his wife, and my five-year-old niece stood eagerly, waiting to see me with a home-cooked chicken in their hands. Deep within, I braced myself for spiritual warfare that required nothing short of a divine infusion of strength. I took a deep breath and proceeded to receive them.

The visit, not verbatim but to the best of my recollection, began with my uncle. He basically pleaded, "Sarah, you're killing your parents with this trouble." He relayed incidences where he thought that my trouble was putting undue stress on mom and daddy to the extent that I was causing them to age prematurely. I would be the cause of their death!

Wow! I was hit with the weightiest argument first, spiritual warfare at its best. As with any convincing argument, an ounce of truth is always in the pound of argument. His plea stunned me because my parents are my blue sky. More than any member of my family, I had a strong attachment to my mom and daddy. I simply hung my head down as the tears rolled off my cheeks and thought, *Lord, I cannot deny your call in my life, but I find myself in a hard place.* I then prayed to Jesus to keep me strong.

Next came my brother, "Every time Chinese New Year comes, Daddy is sad because of you. You can make him happy by coming home and stopping this nonsense." Then his final salvo was, "You see, only your family is here visiting you. Where is your church?"

Continued silence met this unjust criticism.

Finally, my five-year-old niece took hold of my hand and cried, "Auntie, auntie, I miss you. I want to play games with you like before."

My heart broke within, and the emotional burden was far more than I could bear. *Lord Jesus, help me! This is too hard for me to bear!* I prayed silently. The tears from her little face were melting away my heart, but when I was the weakest at that moment, I felt a renewed conviction of my calling, and I would not be deterred from my Lord's will in my life.

I responded to her pleas with a painful silence.

# What Do You Think?

Many of us would like to know in advance that we could pass tests of this magnitude with relative ease, but His provision of strength didn't come until the moment it was needed. Do you have an upcoming situation that will demand His strength to make it through? Trust Him because His answer will come at the right time.

Today's Reflection

_____
_____
_____
_____
_____
_____
_____
_____
_____
_____
_____
_____
_____
_____

Today's Prayer

_____
_____
_____
_____
_____

# Second Arrest and Labor Camp

Day 11

# Not If but When, A Vision from God

"We must go through many hardships to enter the kingdom of God," they said.

—Acts 14:22b

---

After being released from county jail, I rested at my home for three weeks. I was growing eager to reunite with my church family and get back to the ministry of evangelism.

Departing from home was easier said than done. My family suspected I would depart for the ministry and continue following Jesus Christ. I wrote a letter to my family, telling them that living for Christ was the only thing worth living for, which they interpreted as a suicide gesture.

My niece was assigned to be my constant companion and sleeping partner. One night, I left a letter and secretly returned to my church. My brother suspected suicide and began searching for me. When I was nowhere to be found, he desperately jumped into the pond in front of my house, thinking I had drowned myself. They eventually learned I had returned to my church and suicide was not on my mind.

Once reunited with my church family, I underwent forty-five days of intensive Bible studies and strategy sessions. Overdue for a rest, I took a trip to visit with my coworker and the senior pastor. While in transit to their location by bus, I had what I now call a vision, but then it was a persistent impression.

I was walking through a path that was leading to a bridge, and I was eyeing the underpass for shelter. A storm was raging with gusts of wind and sheets of rain battering upon me.

As I reflected on my vision, I felt a profound loneliness. This vision repeated itself while I was en route to my coworker and pastor. I was unable to shake the image from my memory.

I want to incur a brief excursion to my thinking back then. Only the Bible prophets, not simple and common people, had visions. I dare not suggest that I had a similar experience as that of the prophets. That would be arrogant and grandiose of me. Besides, our teaching back then was quite strict on this point. Many abuses have admittedly been done in the name of the Lord, for example, visions, voices, impression, and so forth. But I have come to learn that, with a discerning spirit, abuse does not cancel out right use.

The next day, a local evangelist and I joined in a monthly leadership meeting, encouraging the saints, and breaking bread together. We planned our next day's activities and prepared for bed after prayer. While brushing our teeth, we heard a loud commotion downstairs, shouting and scuffling.

At first, I thought it was a family dispute but quickly realized it was a police raid. We rushed to retrieve our Bibles, and when we reached the door to make our escape, a police officer blocked our way. He immediately handcuffed us and dragged us downstairs. After a while, we were forced to walk to the police station some twenty minutes away.

The next day, I and another coworker were sent to *Sha Yang (The Mouth of the Tiger)* again. While in transport, a breakthrough in my thinking occurred. The vision I had experienced was one of warning and preparation for what was to come, which was happening to me at that very moment. That answer broke through my confusion. I was at peace and settled in the Lord for what was to come.

Hardships are inevitable and inescapable, and how sweet it is to be warned and carried through the hardships by the One who cares for the details of our life.

# What Do You Think?

We may feel alone in our hardships as we pursue the things of God's kingdom, but are we ever really alone? Since our Lord Jesus is a living Lord, He can lift us up when hardships beat us down, and He can make us rise again in triumph as we move to the gates of His kingdom.

Today's Reflection

_____

_____

_____

_____

_____

_____

_____

_____

_____

_____

_____

_____

_____

_____

_____

Today's Prayer

_____

_____

_____

Day 12

# Alone or Together?

They arrested the apostles and
put them in the public jail.

—Acts 5:18

---

**W**hat I'm about to explain took place between being brought to the police station and transferred to *Sha Yang (The Mouth of the Tiger)*. As in the book of Acts, wherever the gospel goes within a hostile power structure, Christians find themselves being arrested, a story that begins with the apostles and continues with regular Christians throughout history and the world. What follows is my story of my second arrest.

After being forced to walk to the station, the officer in charge took Sister Sheng Mei and me and brought us to a secured yard where we were gathered with other sisters and brothers who were rounded up that same night.

He commanded that I bow down before him, an act I was unwilling to fulfill because I reasoned that his command was to demonstrate his dominance over us and was not good police work. It was as though he wanted us to worship him, an idea repugnant to my spirit.

I stood my ground and remained silent. He became furious at my unwillingness to obey his command. He took hold of a nearby broom and began beating us with it until we were forced to the ground from the blows. We were eventually isolated from the others, and he took Sister Sheng Mei and me and handcuffed us to the railing of an inner stairwell on the second floor.

Left to ourselves, we prayed and asked the Lord to help us. He went upstairs, and for the longest time, he had not returned. We both listened intently in order to discover his whereabouts on the floor above us. We slowly realized that he might have gone to sleep. After all, it was the early hours of the morning.

I prayed and asked the Lord to bring a deep sleep upon him, and it was not long until we heard the low sound of snoring above us. I took this as a prayer answered and knew that God wanted us to escape. Sheng Mei was not of the same mind for fear of being caught.

I was able to slip my hand out of the one set of handcuffs that bound us together, making it possible for Sheng Mei to also be released. We discussed what this could mean in low whispers. I eventually tiptoed quietly downstairs to see what activity or guards were there.

To my surprise, no one was to be found. The first floor was completely unoccupied. I signaled to Sheng Mei to come down, and together, we slipped out into the secured courtyard where we were detained earlier. There, we found another sister handcuffed to a tree, but we could not set her free, try as hard as we could.

In the corner of the yard was a bathroom without a ceiling or roof, giving us access to the outer wall. Sheng Mei and I hurried into the bathroom, and I stood on her shoulders. Once on the top of the wall, I turned to reach for her. She said, "You go, I will stay." "No," I whispered, "If they discover I have escaped they will hold you responsible and beat you to death. Come with me! We could escape. This city is familiar to us." I whispered again, "Perhaps God has made a way?"

"No," she insisted.

I tried to reason with her that, if we did not escape, prison would be inevitable. I could not dissuade her. So much to her surprise, I climbed back down from the wall. We were in this together, come what may.

We made our way back to the stairwell, and I slipped my wrist back into the handcuffs and waited for morning to come.

# What Do You Think?

Have you experienced life possibilities before you and not been of the same mind as others who could be affected? What should you do? Who should relent? For me, jail is nowhere for sisters to be alone. It's better to be together than alone in our different directions.

Today's Reflection

_____
_____
_____
_____
_____
_____
_____
_____
_____
_____
_____
_____
_____
_____
_____
_____
_____

Today's Prayer

_____
_____
_____

# Sent to Lao Jiao

Day 13

# Respect and Disrespect

But seek first his kingdom and his righteousness,
and all these things will be given to you as well.
—Matthew 6:33

---

"Sarah," said the guard, "you have visitors ... again!"

Prison culture is very much concerned with outward appearances. For example: How many visits do you get per month? What did they give during your visit? How much money did they leave you with for living extras?

All these things constituted my worth in the eyes of my fellow prisoners and guards. To them, the total sum of life is what you have, for example, clothes, money, friends, and family. If you have these things, you are highly respected and admired. On several occasions after I would return to my dorm, my fellow inmates would surround me, only to be flattered or fussed over. Some even did some of my chores so they could participate in my gifts that my family and friends gave.

Some very tough and powerful inmates took me into their care. When we would line up for a meal, say, breakfast, and I found myself at the end of the line, they would call out to me in the presence of all the other inmates for me to join them at the head of the line, soliciting the ire of those inmates ahead of me. But the inmate leaders would snarl at them, and they would cower in their places.

They respected me not for who I was but from what they could get. Prison culture was very hard to navigate as a Christian because my worth was not from things I wore, ate, or drank. My worth is soundly found in Him, who loves me and cares for me. The things they valued, I did not. The things they strove for, I did not.

Both guards and inmates alike thought me strange for not using my favored position more efficiently as I could. But in my heart, I was confident that the Lord would provide what I needed in the measure I needed it. Their fleeting friendship was based on material items. His love and care for me is based simply in Himself for me. Who could possibly want more?

# What Do You Think?

Have others ever used you for what they can get from you? Or have you ever used others for your ends? Do you agree that, beyond all material things, He is sufficient for us?

Today's Reflection

_____
_____
_____
_____
_____
_____
_____
_____
_____
_____
_____
_____
_____
_____
_____
_____

Today's Prayer

_____
_____
_____
_____
_____

Day 14

# Four Sisters, Three Reasons

By this everyone will know that you are
my disciples, if you love one another.
—John 13:35

———————

"You will meet some of your sisters in Liao Jiao," the officer said to me as I was being transported to my next destination. He went on to say, "So you can take care of them."

*What an odd thing for him to say to me*, I thought
At *Liao Jiao* (Reeducation through Labor Camp), human rights advocates sometimes refer to it as "slavery in the twenty-first century." (See Al Jazeera.) I found myself with four wonderful sisters in Christ and members of my home church: Li Mei, Jiao Zheng, Zhen Mei, and Zhao Xiu (my special auntie). Though our sentences overlapped, we had the privilege of being together for over one year.

I would ask the Lord, "Why am I here?"

It seemed such a waste of time to me. The Lord showed me how necessary it was for the five of us to be together. Here are three main reasons:

First, we helped each other. Since I was a new prisoner unaccustomed to prison work quotas, my sisters stepped in to help. When assembling headphones, they would often pass my workstation and stealthily add to my output from their own workstations so I would not face severe penalties for failing to meet my quota. I marveled at their sacrificial love. They were wonderful examples.

On another occasion, I raced back to the dorm to grab my bowl and spoon for the dinner hour. As I reached for my storage box, I found a generous supply of peanuts and dried salty mustard plant, gifts from my sisters, small but meaningful acts of God's love. I prayed, "Thank you, Jesus, for my precious sisters!"

Second reason was fellowship. During our work hours, all we had to do was give each other the look, and that would mean that we would meet at the restroom area, far removed from the work area. Once we converged in the restroom, we would enter stalls next to each other and quietly pass notes back and forth. The notes would generally be Bible verses, news from home, or concern for another sister's well-being. These brief, silent encounters gave us the strength to go on. We decided to all fast on particular days of the week and speak Bible verses to ourselves daily. In these ways, we encouraged and built each other up in the Lord.

The prison conducted a cleaning campaign every three months. My sisters would take advantage of these times and coordinate a washing trough meeting. These simple moments became sacred moments as we would pray for each other. When one of us was down, the others lifted her up before the Lord and vice versa.

Finally, the Lord used us for evangelism. My mom would smuggle in witnessing booklets, and I would share with my unbelieving friends until the guards confiscated our "dangerous contraband." We would teach our inmates the songs of the church and explained the scriptures to them. This was especially true when we were forced to make carpets. Four prisoners were assigned to make one handwoven carpet. My unbelieving friends and I had plenty of opportunity to talk about God. They were curious about the faith, and we Christians were eager to share the love of our Lord. I look back on those days with great fondness, and I am thankful to Jesus for putting us together. It made bitter days sweet and full of meaning. His love in and through us was a beacon of light in a very dark place.

# What Do You Think?

Do you believe God has a purpose for you, even in the worst of circumstances? How can you show the love of Jesus in those difficult circumstances?

Today's Reflection

_____
_____
_____
_____
_____
_____
_____
_____
_____
_____
_____
_____
_____
_____
_____
_____
_____

Today's Prayer

_____
_____
_____
_____
_____

Day 15

# I Was Lost but Now I'm Found

On their second visit, Joseph told his brothers who
he was,and Pharaoh learned about Joseph's family.
—Acts 7:13

———————

My family suspected I had committed suicide (see
Day 11) but there was always the hope that such
was not true. Just when it seemed all but certain
that I was gone, my third brother thought he saw
me going into a restaurant as he walked along with
his colleagues. Instead of breaking away from his
friends, they all went back to their apartments. He,
however, hurried back to where he thought he saw
me, only to discover it was someone who looked like
me.

This began a number of Sarah sightings by others
when, all the while, I was in labor camp, working
in an off-site carpet mill down from the main labor
camp facility. All my family began to search for me,
and their hope of finding me was renewed.

My brother, the one who suspected I committed
suicide but never fully accepted that explanation in
his heart of hearts, desperately sought me out by
chance at an unmarked facility (because labor camps
are not publicized), inquiring about me.

To his amazement, the guards gladly received him and told him I was at the camp. They asked if he wanted to visit me at that moment. Though unprepared and without gifts in hand, he openly accepted the invitation.

The guards came to me and ordered me to follow them. I complied with the order, and as we exited the carpet mill, I saw my brother at a distance, and he saw me. My brother hurried to me, and we stood close together. Embracing in my culture is not permitted, even in moments like these. With tears running down his face and I with complicated feelings, emotion came over us both as we stood close to each other.

The guards invited us inside the mill, where we could be sheltered from the cold winter day. We sat close to each other. With unceasing crying and unrelenting tears, we communicated our deep love for each other and undying family devotion. Like Joseph meeting his family and being overcome with emotion, so was I. The Lord used my family to be my comfort at a time when I was numb with loneliness.

# What Do You Think?

How has the Lord used your family or unbelieving friends to lift your spirit? Who in your family would you like to give thanks for?

Today's Reflection

_____
_____
_____
_____
_____
_____
_____
_____
_____
_____
_____
_____
_____
_____
_____

Today's Prayer

_____
_____
_____
_____
_____

# My Special Auntie

Peter went with them, and when he arrived
he was taken upstairs to the room. All the
widows stood around him, crying and showing
him the robes and other clothing that Dorcas
had made while she was still with them.

—Acts 9:39

---

"I'll be right here until you close your eyes in sleep,"
she said.

Her love for the Lord and me was truly heaven-sent. This was my special auntie. The term *auntie* is a term of endearment that is both affectionate and respectful. It does not necessarily mean a blood relative, but one who is loved and respected as if she were.

My special auntie was from my home church, and she was my elder by some thirty years. She was already in the labor camp long before I arrived. As you can imagine, the moment we met was an occasion of great joy and comfort. The Lord Jesus would use my auntie to bring special blessing and aid to my life in prison. She was my Dorcas. Just as the widows in Acts 9:39 showed Peter all the wonderful works of Dorcas, so I will show off the wonderful works of love from my special auntie.

As a newcomer in the labor camp, Auntie immediately took it upon herself to help and protect me. She later told me she was honored to care for me because I was an evangelist. I told people about Jesus, and she was just a housewife who served the church with hospitality. Here are a few of the ways that she helped and protected me:

In the early morning hours, while it was still dark, all prisoners were waking up and getting ready for a meager breakfast, a meal slightly above having nothing to eat at all. Then it was off to the work camps. My auntie, because the guards were brutal to any prisoner running late, would rush to my side with water and toothbrush in hand for me to use while she made my bed. We would rush out in time to make roll call in the freezing cold. She had a knack for getting through the food line and out in plenty of time for work duties. Because of her ability to survey the prison environment and make the most of it, she made my life enormously easier.

All during the day, she would look in on me, and we would steal away moments of fellowship and prayer. At night, as we returned from fifteen to eighteen hours of forced labor, she would quickly dart away as I made my way slowly to our prison dorm. When I would arrive, she would have my bed turned down with hot tea prepared and the bed warming with a makeshift hot water bottle.

*How could this be?* I thought. *She does more work than I do!*

Auntie possessed the love, energy, and sagacity that would welcome me back to the dorm with all the humble comforts of prison.

I would plop down on my bed (rack) in total exhaustion, and she would be warming my bitterly cold legs and feet by massaging them back to life. *What kind of woman is this?* I would marvel. *So selfless and genuinely caring.* I could never repay her for her works of service for me.

The day of her release was soon, and the guards had commanded her to gather her things together for her discharge. Strangely, she went about her business as usual. Even the other prisoners, who were excited about her release, were a bit perplexed.

"She doesn't act like she's happy or excited," they would whisper among themselves.

Finally, the day of release had come, and the guards came to escort her out of the dorm. She refused to go. The situation was much more complicated than this. (See Day 17)

She said, "Sarah is more important than I am. She tells people about the love of God. I want to stay and finish her time, and I ask you to let her go in my place."

The guards were stunned, not believing what they were hearing. "What?" they exclaimed. "That is impossible!"

And my special auntie continued to make a case for my release and her continued imprisonment, but it was to no avail.

If the widows of Lydda rightly boasted of the great acts of love Dorcas had done for them while alive, how much more can I boast about my special auntie?

# What Do You Think?

Who in your life has been a Dorcas or special auntie who has clearly demonstrated God's love in sacrificial action? Why not take a moment again to give thanks for shining lights in a sometimes dark world?

Today's Reflection

_____
_____
_____
_____
_____
_____
_____
_____
_____
_____
_____
_____
_____
_____
_____
_____

Today's Prayer

_____
_____
_____
_____

# Peter's Angel, My Auntie

Suddenly an angel of the Lord appeared and
a light shone in the cell. He struck Peter on
the side and woke him up."Quick, get up!" he
said, and the chains fell off Peter's wrists.

—Acts 12:7

---

I will try to unravel the complexities of my auntie's
insistence that she finish out my sentence and I be
released.

In Liao Jiao, good behavior is rewarded every
month by reducing one's sentences by one to three
days, that is, if you have learned your lessons and
allowed yourself to be reeducated. Since we sisters
never repented, we just assumed we were going
to live out our entire sentence. We never bothered
looking at the good behavior board to see if our
sentences were reduced. Strangely, they gave us time
off for simple good behavior and not repentance. So
my dear auntie was being released early. The day of
our release was uncertain even though we counted
the days ourselves. Our calculation didn't make any
provision for good behavior.

From the day my auntie heard she was being
discharged, she began fasting before the Lord,

praying that I should be released and the prison authorities would accept her request of exchange. After five days of fasting, officials stopped her and told her to prepare for discharge and not go to the fields or factory to work. My auntie put the offer of exchange before them. Stunned by her response, they unequivocally denied her request. And Auntie made another impassioned plea for my release, and after much intense discussion, yet to no avail, she flatly refused to go home and emphatically told them to release me.

"We see reeducation through labor has failed!" they shouted back.

She begged them to listen to her reasons. "Jesus saved me from my sins, and I owe Him all my life. Sarah can do much more for God than I can. Please let her go and do God's will. Jesus has also healed me from cancer. Even though I had no money or help from anyone, I cried out to God, and He healed me. I stand here as a testimony to His power. Please let Sarah go."

They physically picked her up and dragged her out of the main compound, where she quickly made her way back inside. They brought in the prison educator to persuade her to leave, but Auntie was convinced that my release and her continued imprisonment was the right thing to do.

Finally, the prison warden was brought in to resolve the impasse. He quickly perceived that Auntie was bent on living out my sentence. The educator and warden were convinced that I was a ringleader of the

Christians and I was manipulating this simpleminded woman to take my place.

An official was sent to the factory where I was working, and she took me aside and sternly told me to talk Auntie into leaving as she should. Then she threatened me, "If you do not persuade her to leave, we will put both of you in the hole!"

This frightened me because the hole is a form of torture.

I talked with Auntie and told her, "It's not working!"

But Auntie insisted that my release would mean more people coming to God. "They must let you go!"

I knew then that my attempt to persuade her failed.

That night, we sat up together and prepared ourselves for the hole. We layered our clothes and asked others to watch our belongings until we were released from confinement.

The next day, we didn't go to the hole. We simply went about our regular duties.

On a cold, rainy day, the guards again rushed her and dragged her out of the prison and the main gate. *There*, they thought, *we have rid ourselves of her. We've complied with our orders!*

Once outside the main gate, she raced to the factory, where we were busy at our work. The officer of the day was amazed to see her show up at her factory. She gave me one more opportunity to persuade her to leave, which failed of course. In her anger, the officer called upon other willing inmates to pick up Auntie and throw her out of her factory and lock the door behind her.

That was the last time I saw Auntie until the Lord brought us back together again two years later. Tears of love and joy were the only way I could describe our blessed reunion. Peter had his angel, and I had my auntie.

# What Do You Think?

Besides Jesus, is there anyone who would sacrifice for your well-being? Is there anyone that you would be Auntie to?

Today's Reflection

_____
_____
_____
_____
_____
_____
_____
_____
_____
_____
_____
_____
_____
_____
_____
_____

Today's Prayer

_____
_____
_____
_____
_____

Day 18

# Pearls before Pigs?

Do not give dogs what is sacred; do not throw your
pearls to pigs. If you do, they may trample them
under their feet, and turn and tear you to pieces."
—Matthew 7:6

---

In today's politically correct media and culture,
Jesus' words would be offensive. But to us, who
have embraced His love and salvation, we profoundly
value His every word. It is not offensive.

On a particular visit to *Liao Jiao*, my dear mom
smuggled a New Testament to me.

During visiting times, under the watchful eye of
the guards, they would monitor our every move, so
timing is everything. The moment the guard was
distracted and turned around, my sweet mother
stealthily handed off the Bible to me, which I instantly
hid inside my shoe. My dear mother knew exactly
what I needed, and as has been the story of her life,
she provided life's essentials at just the right time.

Unfortunately, I had to maintain vigilance in
guarding that which we believers valued above all
else, His Word. We were constantly subjected to
surprise inspections while we were away performing
our work duties. When we would return late in the

evening, after a long day, we would find all of our belongings and beds turned over and strewn across the dorm. The guards sought out anything of value, personal items, or criminal paraphernalia, like drugs or a Bible.

Since Jesus taught us to be as shrewd as serpents and gentle as doves, I hid my Bible outside, inside a storm drain. But I could see rain was on its way one day, so to protect my valued possession, I withdrew it from its hiding place and dug a hole in the ground, just rear of the kitchen in a grassy area. *Good*, thought I, *a safe place for God's treasured Word.*

That day, the gardening crew was ordered to clear out the grassy area of all growth. Using a hoe, they tilled up the soil. My auntie was a part of this cleanup crew and witnessed a fellow inmate uncover my hidden treasure. This worker snatched up the Bible and hid it in her bosom. Afterward the crew was sent to the pig stalls to clean up around them. There, she opened the Bible, only to find cash inside. She grabbed at the cash and discarded the Bible as if it had no value.

Auntie saw it all and retrieved the Bible when it was safe to do so. She lovingly and tenderly returned the Bible into my trust. It's hard to explain the inestimable worth of God's Word. And to think the worker stole the cash, which is of temporal worth, and discarded God's eternal Word as worthless. The values of God's people sure look strange to an unbelieving world.

# What Do You Think?

What other values do you think separate us from the world? How should we act when it appears our values are being trampled?

Today's Reflection

_____

_____

_____

_____

_____

_____

_____

_____

_____

_____

_____

_____

_____

_____

Today's Prayer

_____

_____

_____

_____

_____

# Tomorrow, You Will Be Released!

Now, Lord, consider their threats and enable your servants to speak your word with great boldness.

—Acts 4.29

---

Though my personal experience overtly lacks the miraculous of Peter's escape of Acts 4, it nevertheless was miraculous in my eyes.

A week before my discharge, my brother engaged the prison authority to inquire about my release date and time. After some delay, they replied that I would be released on such and such date and time. This was exciting news to me. I knew my release day was close, but now I know exactly when it would transpire.

"Tomorrow, I will be released," was my incredulous mantra.

Then a guard sent word to me that I was to go to the discharge officer's area for a release appointment. During my visit with the discharge officer, she pressed me on my immediate future plans. "I'm not sure" I replied. "Will you still believe in Jesus?" she continued, "Of course" I answered.

Finally in an impatient manner, she forcefully insisted "You are not to return to the church. If you do, you will be rearrested!"

*A warning or threat*, thought I. *Never mind, I would serve the Lord no matter what.* Outwardly, I offered not a word.

Excited and anxious all at once best described my emotional state that night after my visit with the discharge officer. On the one hand, I would be rejoined to my dear family, celebrating my newfound freedom with the people I loved deeply. Then on the other hand, I feared the moment I would tell my family that I would be returning to the church to resume my duty as an evangelist, a meeting that would bring about a familial upheaval.

Back in my dormitory for my last night, friends—both Christian and not—came by to say their good-byes and Godspeeds. There was an air of happiness for my imminent release, along with good-natured envy and sadness as they anticipated my absence.

O what a night, a sleepless one! Thoughts of the future raced through my head and heart. *What will tomorrow bring?*

Then I remembered that I hid a hundred yuan (approximately seventeen US dollars) that my family gave to me, inside my handmade quilt, over a span of my prison time. So I frantically searched for it. My quilt was stuffed with seedless raw cotton, and grasping here and there, I slowly realized that my money was missing. *Where can it be?* I searched my memory. *Was it stolen, misplaced, or what?*

The reality that it was missing settled in, but my imminent release made the bitter loss bearable. *My Bible! Who will get my Bible?* I thought. Instantly, a dear non-Christian friend came to mind. She was the lead trustee of gardening. I gave her my most treasured gift, and she was most grateful.

"Lord, Jesus may Your Word accomplish Your will in her," is still my prayer.

The morning couldn't come quick enough, and when it arrived, it was sunshine and happiness. The prison morning routine was as it has always been until everyone was sent to the work details. Saying my last good-byes and the emotional roller coaster I was on was coming to a head. *It's quiet, so very quiet*, I thought to myself.

I was out of my dorm and escorted to the discharge staging area near the main gate. Then after I was called in for one last discussion, officials sternly admonished me to avoid God, religion, and the church.

Then they asked me, "Will you still believe in Jesus?"

I unflinchingly answered, "Yes."

My response disturbed them, but they were resigned to the fact that I had fulfilled my sentence and nothing more could be done.

Then the gates slowly opened, and I could begin to make out my brother's form. Then as the gates were fully opened, there he stood with a motorcycle, prepared to whisk me home. Free at last, I would be riding home on his motorcycle with the sun in my face and the wind in my hair. With mixed emotions and every passing minute, it took me further from my captivity.

Overwhelmed by God's goodness, I could not speak. A hypersensitivity to the Spirit was my state of mind, and constant communing was my comfort. I wanted Jesus to use me like never before. My resolve, as in Acts 4:29, was, "God, use me with great boldness!"

# What Do You Think?

After being tested by the Lord, are you tempted to withdraw or retire from His service? Or can you, like the early church, say, "Enable your servants with great boldness"?

Today's Reflection

_____

_____

_____

_____

_____

_____

_____

_____

_____

_____

_____

_____

_____

_____

_____

_____

Today's Prayer

_____

_____

_____

_____

_____

Day 20

# My Family and the Gospel Field

Jesus replied, "No one who puts a hand
to the plow and looks back  is fit for
service in the kingdom of God."
—Luke 9:62

---

Words can never express the gratitude I have for my family and all they did for me while I was in prison and upon my release. God used them as a healing balm for my soul. Their love and care for me was humbling and quite undeserved. I will be forever grateful to them.

My first night home, my family gathered all our relatives for a big celebration. The house was made ready, chicken and duck with all the trimmings were prepared, and the atmosphere was exuberant. Except that deep in my soul, I feared that, not long from now, all would come crashing in because I longed to return to the church and my field of ministry. But tonight, I wanted to we celebrate with no discussion of my future plans.

"Little sister is home! Let's plan her future!" eventually became the topic of discussion.

*Should I tell them what is in my heart? No, not tonight,* I thought. So as they busily made plans for my tomorrows, I sat quietly by realizing this was going to be difficult. *Lord Jesus, help me to do Your will!*

After two weeks at home and enjoying familiar surroundings, I wanted to reciprocate with my family for all they had done for me. I felt so indebted to them. I asked if I could help with the cotton harvest, and they permitted me to participate in the harvesting of the cotton petals after the cotton was already picked. I was happy to help in the family business and be a contributing member once again.

By day, I was able to help in the labor. By night, I wrestled with anxiety, knowing that all this would end as I had chosen to put my hands to the plow in God's harvest field, my beloved China. *Painful to stay, painful to leave*, was my inner anticipation.

If I stayed with my family, I would be forfeiting the call of Jesus in my life to follow Him in the gospel field. It was a possibility I could not entertain, not because I feared a wrathful God but because He gave all to me. His love compels me to follow. If I left to return to the gospel field, the pain of separation would be overwhelming. It would require nothing short of a miracle to endure the pain, a marvel I believed that He would provide.

One day, my sister-in-law was about to head out to the cotton fields for harvesting. This time, I asked if I could join in the harvest. She said yes, and I could see how happy we all were to have our family back together.

During the harvesting, we took some time to talk together. She was quick to point out how happy the family was to have Little Sister back and doing well. She also said that I should not be concerned about what villagers might say about me. After all, I was the only person ever in the entire village to do prison time. In short, I had gained an infamous reputation among the locals, and my sweet sister-in-law was assuring me that family love would overcome community embarrassment.

I have to admit that what the villagers thought never entered my mind. To hear my sister-in-law talk like this was so foreign to me. It even felt surreal. I have never considered myself to be a criminal, but rather, only as one suffering for Christ. My personal reputation was of no concern to me, let alone to distant others.

She went on to relate to me how my brother (her husband) had come to life again since I had returned these two weeks.

"He is happier than I have ever seen him," she reported with her own appreciative contentment. She gave me detailed examples of his newfound happiness, "He sings and whistles throughout the day. We're all so glad you are with us again."

My sister-in-law was being so transparent, openhearted, and sincere, and within me, I knew that now was the moment I had to speak up. But what do you say to someone who openly and unpretentiously shares her heart with you? Love makes it harder, not easier, to do His will. But I was committed to do His will.

I broke my silence in this extremely emotionally vulnerable moment. I told her of my plans to return to the gospel field and finish the mission Jesus gave me to do.

In utter disbelief and shock, my dear sister-in-law, in tears and wailing, was bowing down before me, begging me not to leave. "It will break your brother's heart!" she cried with unceasing tears. "It will break everyone's heart!"

Our harvesting ended abruptly, and we quietly made our way home.

That night, they held a family intervention meeting with the goal of getting me to stay with the family and not go the way of harm and prison again. After they all pleaded their case, they saw that, although moved emotionally, I was determined to rejoin my church family.

Their disappointment turned to anger, which they directed to my mom.

"If only you didn't make her go to church with you!" they shouted at her. "See what you have done. You've ruined her young life. What will become of her?"

But my mom defended herself by asserting "What? She is an adult. I didn't force to do anything she didn't choose to do."

But anger would not be appeased, and at one point, she was shoved and told, "You, an old woman, have destroyed Sarah's young life!"

I assured my family that it was not Mom's fault. What she had done for me by bringing me to Christ was the greatest gift. In my heart of hearts, the ministry that Jesus called me to was an unfinished mission. I must return to the gospel field immediately!

Threats were aimed at me. "We will not visit you in prison anymore!" they retorted.

My heart was breaking. They loved me deeply, and they thought they were doing the right thing, but in the end, we all went our separate ways in exasperation that night.

*The moon was so full and bright that night,* thought I.

Yet my heart was shattered. I cried to the Lord for the pain was overwhelmingly great. In the doorway of my home, as I stared up to the moon, the floodgates of tears flowed until I could cry no more. Then I quietly retired for the night. The Comforter came with only the comfort He could provide.

At sunrise, I packed quickly and modestly turned to say good-bye to my family. I first went to my daddy.

With his heart breaking, he begged me, "Listen to me just this once!"

I respectfully listened to his final plea, to which I affirmed my love to him but expressed that I was determined to do God's will in this matter.

Emotion overcame my much-loved sister-in-law that she fainted and we carried her to her bed. At which time, I turned to my brother and braced myself for one last torrent of challenge.

My brother, my always faithful sibling, said in the mildest way, "I will always be your brother. No matter where you go, I will be there for you."

And with that, I turned with bag in hand and left the room. I walked out of the house and went to the bus station. Then the bus hurried me to my new destination, the field of God, where I put my hands to the plow, trusting he would make me fit for His service. And he did.

# What Do You Think?

Have you or do you anticipate that you will one day have to make heart-wrenching decisions to serve the Lord? Pray now for His strength because He hears and answers the heart's cry.

Today's Reflection

_____

_____

_____

_____

_____

_____

_____

_____

_____

_____

_____

_____

_____

_____

_____

Today's Prayer

_____

_____

_____

_____

# Third Arrest and Labor Camp ... Again

# Slapped but Not Silenced

Paul looked straight at the Sanhedrin and said,
"My brothers, I have fulfilled my duty to God
in all good conscience to this day." At this the
high priest Ananias ordered those standing
near Paul to strike him on the mouth.

Acts 23:1-2

---

Once I had reconnected with the church, we immediately were off to an evangelist retreat, where all the regional workers came together for prayer, worship, study, and refreshment. What a celebration it was. I was back where I was supposed to be, in the midst of the church family preparing for the ministry once again. It was sweet fellowship with God and my coworkers. And not long afterward, it was back out into the field again. I had the privilege of revisiting and renewing many friendships from the past. What a glorious time to be alive!

About three years later, I was involved in a magazine ministry that was designed to teach, edify, and encourage both believer and unbeliever alike.

While in Zhong Xiang city, my coworker and I were at the home of a member of our church when we received word that Sister Li Ying was arrested along with her host family. All of them, including a three-year-old child, were hauled into custody.

Such news, as you can imagine, caused great alarm among the rest of us in the city.

*Were the police looking for the rest of us? Was this the beginning of a new crackdown?* We thought immediately. *If so, we must hide our computers and other high-value assets of the magazine ministry.*

We hurriedly packed up our magazine assets out of fear of imminent danger and shipped all our ministry items far away, out of harm's way of confiscation. After securing our ministry items, we stealthily rushed back to our host homes, avoiding detection by police and would-be informants. My thoughts raced to the plight of my dear Sister Li Ying and her host family, who were only demonstrating the love of Jesus by showing her hospitality. *What would become of them?* Such thoughts occupied me, only being too familiar firsthand with the cruelty of the Chinese government toward the good people of God.

Safe in the home of our brave hosts, we dined together, and my coworker and I prepared for bed, feeling relatively secure.

Near midnight, the dog began to bark wildly. I woke up out of my sleep to hear the home being broken in on all sides and through the roof.

Since we were all lodging in the first level, my coworker and I raced upstairs, and the host family tried to delay and distract the police so we could make our getaway. All in all, about seventy-five police officers were involved in that raid. Thank God, all our ministry equipment was not to be found!

Unfortunately, we were located and immediately handcuffed. Everything in the home was confiscated: furniture, Bibles, books, money, and whatever else in their reach. The house was left bare, and everyone was taken into custody.

My coworker and I were placed in the same police car.

Once in the police car, my coworker calmly protested the arrest by saying, "We only believe in Jesus. Why do you treat us like serious criminals?"

The police officer answered her by brutally striking her across the face. We silently prayed, "Lord Jesus, protect us from this injustice."

We were taken to the closest police facility available at that time, a police academy for new recruits. This facility was not designed to incarcerate prisoners, but it would suffice for the moment.

We were separated not long after our arrival. She was taken in shackles into a courtyard, and I was dragged off to a basement. We were close enough to hear each other's cries of pain and torture. To hear my coworker was as painful as the brutality forced upon me. I can honestly say we shared each other's pain, and we both shared in the suffering of Christ, who endured far more than we could imagine or think.

When my coworker was slapped in the face and the two of us were later beaten and tortured for the faith, we both were brought to a crossroad. One direction was marked with anger and bitterness; the other showed peace and providence. We both chose the latter. Our God knew what He was doing.

# What Do You Think?

What painful situation(s) can you recall in which you also reached a crossroad and had to choose between anger and bitterness or peace and God's providence? Describe the process of making that decision.

Today's Reflection

_____
_____
_____
_____
_____
_____
_____
_____
_____
_____
_____
_____
_____
_____
_____
_____

Today's Prayer

_____
_____
_____
_____
_____

# Interrogated

Blessed are those who are persecuted because of righteousness, for theirs is the kingdom of heaven.
—Matthew 5:10

---

I will summarize this event for the benefit of those who have not seen the video, *Sarah's Trail of Blood*, which is available at SarahLiu.sjf@gmail.com.

As stated in Day 21, my coworker and I were arrested and subsequently separated for interrogation. I choose not to go into graphic detail about what transpired during interrogation, other than to say it was extremely painful and deeply humiliating. The instruments they used to inflict pain were hands for slapping and punching, feet for brutally kicking, a book to pound me, and a clothes hanger to beat my body. And the most painful and damaging was an electric baton that would shock and burn my flesh. There was no limit to their evil and perverse imaginations. I can honestly say that the video, *Sarah's Trail of Blood*, is a sanitized and made-for-public-consumption video. It tries to explain the events as discreetly as possible.

The interrogator's goal was to make me sign a confession, implicating my leaders and coworkers and divulging names and locations of key church members and assets.

After two nights and two days of almost nonstop interrogation and torture, they finally realized I was not going to sign the document.

However, I must explain that I had waning moments. I wish I could tell you that I never had the thought of surrender or signing the confession. I wish I could tell you that I was strong every moment they inflicted more and more pain. In actuality, I was barely hanging on or, as the Scripture puts it, "beyond our ability to endure" (2 Cor. 1:8).

But at that moment and in that place, God met me and gave me His strength, and He became my sufficiency. I am painfully aware that I am a sinner. Nevertheless, I am also joyfully aware that I am a sinner saved by grace.

# What Do You Think?

All of us have or will face hardships that test our mettle. Where there is failure, there is also forgiveness. Where there is overcoming, we are crowned with patient endurance. Either way, God is with us.

Today's Reflection

_____
_____
_____
_____
_____
_____
_____
_____
_____
_____
_____
_____
_____
_____
_____
_____
_____
_____

Today's Prayer

_____
_____
_____
_____
_____

# Sent to Jail

Day 23

# Given a Two-Year Sentence

But God was with him and rescued him from all his troubles. He gave Joseph wisdom and enabled him to gain the goodwill of Pharaoh king of Egypt.

—Acts 7:9b–10b

---

I have to admit that it was rare to receive any goodwill from prison officials, but I did receive favor from other prisoners. In jail or prison, goodwill from anybody is a welcome relief. What little favor and goodwill was experienced was an enormous blessing and a fresh touch of human kindness.

When I was finally placed in jail after my brutal interrogation, I was with six sisters from our church who were incarcerated before me. Although genuinely pleased to see each other, we were more concerned about each other's condition.

When I entered the cell, they all rushed to my aid because I was barely able to walk from being shackled the night before and forced to walk throughout the night (see *Sarah's Trail of Blood*). By this time, my feet were acutely swollen with skin coloration turning black and persistent open wounds where the shackles had torn at my ankles. My sisters were shocked at the sight of my condition, beaten, filthy, and in unimaginable pain.

They helped me to a wooden cot where I helplessly collapsed. By day, there was no relief from the flies. And by night, there was no respite from mosquitos. As you can imagine, my condition only worsened even though my sisters tried to care for me with little to no provisions to do so.

A guard looked in on us, and I could tell from the look on his face that he was shocked at my condition. Eventually, I would be transported to a prison hospital. My dear sisters rushed to carry me to the waiting police car. Officials prevented them and forced me to stand to my feet and walk to the transport vehicle under my own power.

I slowly rose and stood on my swollen feet and began the long trek to the waiting car. Bracing myself along every wall and rail, I made it to the police vehical. Once in the car, I thanked the Lord for the strength to accomplish this small task. My dear sisters in Christ felt helpless before the unfeeling guards.

Once at the hospital, I was given immediate emergency treatment, including nutrients intravenously. However, even during this initial treatment, the officers continued to batter me with a barrage of questions, insults, and threats. They even reported to me that Ya Jun, another dear coworker, was in an upper level of the hospital, severely beaten for being uncooperative, a fate that was promised to me if I didn't answer their questions. I remained silent, and my refusal to speak infuriated them all the more.

The attending nurse expressed sorrow and dismay at their treatment of me. "What happened to her ankles?" she snapped at the officers.

"A bad case of mosquito bites!" was their incredulous response.

The nurse didn't buy that for a moment. She turned to me and said with genuine sympathy, "You're only a child, a middle school girl. What possibly could you have done?" She advised, "Tell them something so they would stop this brutal treatment."

The officers silenced her, and then she departed the room murmuring, "So very young."

For the next three days, I was completely immobilized, and with medical care, the swelling began to subside, and I was gradually regaining my strength. Then it was back to jail and to my cell.

When I arrived back in my cell, I found only four of the six sisters still there. No one was quite sure what happened to the other two. We were to later learn that the other two were transported to another facility. The remaining sisters all agreed that the police were trying to divide and conquer. We all vowed to keep silent.

The next day, they took away one of our sisters for interrogation. Sadly, this was an extremely trying time on my dear sister, and we all felt doom in our hearts. Late that night, she was dragged back into the cell, beaten and burned all over her body, and we did all we could to comfort her and tend to her wounds. She told me afterward that the interrogators had mercilessly abused her, but she said that her greatest pain came when they threatened to execute me (Sarah) if she did not speak up and give up the names of key sisters and brothers. She kept silent.

The mood in the cell was sedate and gravely serious. Ominous dark clouds were gathering overhead. But instead of succumbing to fear, we decided to turn to the Lord, our help and refuge. We encouraged each other from Scripture, reminding ourselves that, when Jesus saw the ominous dark clouds of the cross before Him, He went to the Father in prayer. "Yet not as I will, but as you will." Matthew 26.39f.

For the next three days, we fasted and prayed in such a manner and spirit. We believed the Lord prepared us for what was to come. Ominous dark clouds gave way to hope and fearlessness.

As anticipated, I was taken in for interrogation again. I was pulled out of my cell and pushed toward the interrogation room. On the way, I caught sight of the man who hosted my coworker and I just before our arrest. He was on the floor writhing in pain, sobbing aloud. I saw this with my own eyes. I had an overwhelming temptation to succumb to fear, but I overcame with the Lord's help.

My interrogators produced many pictures from our church magazine as other evidence, demanding forcefully to admit to crimes and implicate the brothers. They would yell, "Who do you know?" or "Give us their names!"

I kept silent. This refusal to speak drove them mad. They began to beat me again and again. Then they used an electric baton to torture me. The first application of shock they applied was to the back of my head. I heard the sound of electricity being applied to me, but to my surprise, I felt no pain.

"Lord, is this a miracle for me?" I queried.

But like Peter and the roaring sea, I felt my faith give way and soon began to sink into pain and despair. My interrogators pulled out all the stops. Beatings yielded nothing and electric shock even less. Finally in a desperate attempt, they threatened to rape me and tore at my clothes to show their seriousness. Outside the interrogation rooms was a dog kennel. They threatened to throw me to the dogs and bury me alive afterward.

"No one will ever know!" they would say.

After this ordeal, I was no longer afraid.

Jail time yielded nothing for the officials. They decided to send me to *Jing Men* (Tiger Jail) for a year. I had been sentenced to Jing Men before. At least I knew where I was going and how to get around.

Even though Jing Men has a notorious reputation, I fell into favor with my cellmates. One older woman was imprisoned for violence toward city officials. The other was a middle-aged woman sent up on drug charges. Both took a liking to me. I was their little sister, and we grew fond of each other.

Another favorable turn of events was that the head cook took a liking to us and went out of his way to treat us with special dishes reserved only for the better-off inmates. He had nothing to gain from us. Why was he so kind to us?

Favor, goodwill, and kindness are rare in prison, especially a place like Jing Men. Such moments were like streams of water in the desert or rain to a parched land. This was the Lord's blessing to us. And we took it all in as we went back to our cells.

I heard the familiar voices of my sisters and called out to them. I thanked the Lord for my cellmates, but I was overwhelmed with joy at the sound of my sisters' voices.

Perhaps I did not experience the goodwill from officials as Joseph did; nevertheless, favor, goodwill, and kindness from anyone in Jing Men is to be counted as a blessing. I was blessed, and I had the assurance from Christ that fear would not overtake me again because He is with me.

# What Do You Think?

Have you had acts of kindness, no matter how small, that were assurances to you that Christ is near you? What can you do today that can be that guarantee to another person? Be used of God; let His favor rest on you this day.

Today's Reflection

_____

_____

_____

_____

_____

_____

_____

_____

_____

_____

_____

_____

_____

_____

_____

_____

_____

Today's Prayer

_____

_____

_____

_____

Day 24

# Decision Appealed

When it was daylight, the magistrates
sent their officers to the jailer with
the order: "Release those men."
—Acts 16:35

$A$t this juncture, it may be worth to explain the difference between Laogai and Lao Jiao. The primary purpose of Laogai is to function as a criminal institution (punitive), whereas Lao Jiao functions as a behavior-altering institution (reeducation through labor), hence, reformative. In actuality, the line of difference is blurred. To us prisoners, it was all just prison, and punishment was the state's form of reeducation, albeit labor, labor, and more labor governed by quotas.

Now for the very first time, I entered the inside of a courtroom. I was assigned a court-appointed attorney who was more concerned with befriending the prosecution and the judge than he was with the facts of our case. What was the outcome?

"You are sentenced to two years in Laogai!" The judge handed down to us.

I was stunned. *Two years in a criminal institution for two magazine testimonies?*

Although the difference between Laogai and Lao Jiao might be a matter of degrees, every degree counts! What a significant blow.

After the shock wore off, I submitted a hurried handwritten appeal to the court and eventually won an audience once again with the court. The sentenced was stayed for the moment, and I was not transferred to Laogai.

I, along with sixteen other sisters and brothers, were brought into the appeals court to have our case reconsidered. Upon entering the courtroom, we saw a team of Beijing lawyers that our church hired with the help of Bob Fu and China Aid.

The humble offering of the church touched the Beijing lawyers. They defended us with tenacity and fearlessly.

Partial victory was the outcome. Four were to be released; the remaining thirteen were to be held in custody. I was one of the four.

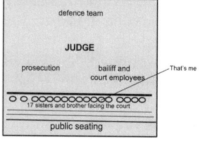

Imagine the scene with me. There we stood before the judge, all seventeen of us adorned with our bright yellow Tiger Prison vests about us. The setting is quite intimidating, yet the Lord comforted us, and the church family, along with China Aid, stood by our side.

During one of the court recesses, families were told to prepare to take their family members away without delay, should they be released.

Finally, the pronouncement came from the bench, "The following prisoners are to be released immediately ... Sarah Liu!"

At the sound of my name, it was as though the noose was cut off a condemned prisoner.

My first response was an overwhelming desire to yell at the top of my lungs, "God is righteous! God is just!"

However, my joy was immediately tempered by the knowledge that most of my sisters and brothers were to remain in chains, and my heart sank once again.

As we departed the court, thirteen were handcuffed, and I and the other three were not restrained, signifying that police and prison agents were observing the court's decision.

"Everyone back to the cars!" the lead officer shouted.

I responded, "But we were released."

Then I thought they were going to transport us back to Tiger Prison to gather our belongings and then release us into the custody of our waiting families.

Once out of the court's view, we were handcuffed and dragged to the cars. Something in the pit of my stomach was telling me that the situation was going awry.

As the caravan of cars began to pull away from the courthouse, families who had waited to receive back their loved ones stood in front of the cars, preventing the caravan from exiting the courthouse parking area. The police pushed back and assaulted the families with electric batons.

Amidst all the chaos, we were welcomed back to Tiger Jail to a hero's welcome. Our fellow prisoners were incredulous.

"How did you beat the charge?" they shouted. "We want your lawyers to defend us too!" they happily exclaimed.

Once returned to our cells, we gathered our belongings, and our cellmates earnestly implored us not to forget about them. We promised they would be prayed for and not forgotten.

In the end, we were called out to sign documents. What an exciting moment, a mere formality. But as I read the document before me, I soon realized that these were not release documents but rather a document acknowledging that we had just been sentenced to Lao Jiao for three years.

"This is a mistake," I protested.

"Shut up and sign the documents," the officer curtly responded.

In utter dismay, I answered, "The court released us. You have to obey the court."

Then fierce and intimidating language spewed out of his mouth, telling me that, whether I signed the document or not, I would be taken to Lao Jiao this very day, and there was nothing and nobody who could change it.

Just when I thought there was some rule of law in China that was dashed to pieces. I reasoned within myself that black is white and white is black. Law means nothing to my beloved China. Oh, the sorrow that came over me, like darkness swallowing me up.

This was clearly a clandestine operation against us—God's righteous verdict and man's stubborn anger. As I look back on this episode, I'm not sure who gave the order to put us away. I conjecture either

- the judge felt that his hand was forced to be lenient, having been visited by such a distinguished team of Beijing lawyers, that he perhaps secretly rescinded his order; *or*
- these backward Christians were not going to outdo the prison officials; *or*
- the clandestine operation was some attempt at selfish ambition to please some superior.

Whatever the motive for this travesty of justice, I was certain God was for us and even this injustice would be rectified in His perfect plan. In the meantime, off to Lao Jiao I would go with the Lord before me and behind me.

# What Do You Think?

Can you recall the last injustice or unwarranted harm that has come to you, through no fault of your own? Whatever that injustice might be, our God is greater than the harm, anger, or despair that might want to rush in and overtake us. The apostle Paul encountered, at least to some degree, just officials. I encountered unjust ones. Circumstances and situations change, but "Jesus Christ is the same yesterday and today and forever." Hebrews 13:8.

Today's Reflection

_____
_____
_____
_____
_____
_____
_____
_____
_____
_____
_____
_____
_____
_____
_____
_____
_____
_____
_____
_____
_____

# Today's Prayer

_____

_____

_____

_____

_____

_____

# Sent to Lao Jiao...again

# Not My First Rodeo!

In his humiliation he was deprived of justice.
—Acts 8:33

---

I had mixed feelings as we drove up to Lao Jiao. On the one hand, after surviving such an unjust ordeal, I was now resolved to go through the next prison episode drawing even closer to God. And on the other, I was sharing the burden of the welfare of my other three sisters.

One emotional consolation of being sent to Lao Jiao was that "it was not my first rodeo," as my American friends would say. Having been at this particular Lao Jiao before gave an experiential advantage over the newbies. Nevertheless, prison is, after all, still prison.

Our police escorts were trying to frighten us by telling us that Lao Jiao's infamous guards had earned their notorious reputation and we should brace ourselves for ill treatment.

Upon our arrival, a lead trustee (a female inmate given oversight authority) rushed out to set the prison tone and tempo. Speaking to us harshly and condescendingly, she demanded that we present all our items before her for inspection.

She immediately seized all of our best items: hygiene supplies and our handmade quilts that our families gave to us. It was humiliating to have her rifle through our items, taking whatever she wanted.

Then out of the guard's view, she conducted a full body search. In my right pocket was my hurried handwritten appeal. As she read through it, a malignant expression came over her face. *What will she do with it?* I thought.

At this moment, the jeering look on her face and the deliberate and intentional shredding of my appeal broke my suspense.

"You will have no need for this here!" she responded cynically.

I protested, "But that's my appeal. I have rights!"

She snarled in return, "Not here you don't. Not here."

Her abuse communicated an I'm-in-charge attitude, and her performance pleased the guards well.

Our police escorts tried to instill fear in us. Then the trustee tried to put us in our place. Now we were being marched in for a haircut. A haircut is too classy a term for what they did. These female barbers were more barbarian than hairdresser.

With twisted and perverted attitudes, they launched into a cutting tirade. It was as though they were blindly hacking away with only one goal in mind, to humiliate us. Because no mirrors were in these rooms, we could only imagine what they were doing to us. As for me, I could feel her hacking at my hair. In some places, she cut close to my scalp.

In other places, she hacked away without design or form. Just then, I remembered the prophecy of Jesus, who was silent as "a lamb to the slaughter." Isaiah 53:7.

"Give me your power, Lord, to endure this humiliation," I prayed.

Then I cried, not for any vanity but for the darkness our Lord endured in the hands of sinful men. With a broken heart, I shared that humiliation in a small way.

After this, we four were separated and assigned to separate cells. Then we were all summoned to an administration office for a special orientation meeting designed with us four in mind.

"This is why you are here ... This is where you will stay ... These are your duties."

So far, we understood what was being expected of us, and it did not appear to be out of the ordinary for Lao Jiao. But now, the other shoe dropped.

They really called us in because we were Christians, and for us, there were special rules. She went on to state unequivocally that we were not permitted to associate with each other from here on out. We were not to pray or pray for anyone else. We were forbidden to tell anyone about Jesus and the gospel, and we could not assemble for religious reasons.

"Do you understand these rules? If you violate any, we will add to your sentence."

Can you imagine the shock and dismay we experienced? We all were consoled by the knowledge that you can intimidate and threaten us, but you can't stop the love of God and the gospel of Christ.

Besides the prohibitions against Jesus, we were told that we had forty-eight hours to memorize some one hundred-plus standard rules of conduct and to ready ourselves for oral examination. The lead trustee administered the examination.

After successfully passing our code of conduct examination, we were then assigned to work details. Off to our work site we went. I was assigned to work in the headphone factory where I estimate a hundred and fifty women worked in terrible conditions. Because of my small hands and nimble fingers, I eventually landed the first station task, which required speed and accuracy because all other stations depended on our output.

I worked feverishly for long hours. Our meals were lacking in nutrition, and we were sleep-deprived while trying to keep up with our quotas. At one point, I collapsed from sheer exhaustion, and the whole operation dramatically slowed. I was literally dragged unconscious from my station to the camp nurse. The inmates fondly called her the "tiger lady" for her cold and uncaring manner.

Once I regained consciousness, the tiger lady asked, "Do you believe in Jesus?"

"I do."

With disgust on her face and without warning, she slapped me, exposing her obvious hate and disapproval of Christ. She went on to deny me any medical attention.

An elderly inmate, who was prison shrewd and worldly wise, came to my rescue. (Of all people to use, Lord.) She rebuked the tiger lady for her abuse and physically carried me to her cell to care for me. Even the hard-bitten guards could see the correctness of my Good Samaritan friend. However, the tiger lady's order still stood, and I was denied any medical relief other than an IV. After being cared for, I was returned to my lead station to resume my duties. At great risks to themselves, my dear sisters in Christ helped me in various and sundry ways.

Though humiliated and denied of justice, the Lord made Himself known every step of the way and at each turn. The mighty hand of God used believer and unbeliever alike to say to me, "Never will I leave you; never will I forsake you." His presence is sweeter than the stench of humiliation and injustice.

# What Do You Think?

Have you found the Lord present in your difficult situations? Have you overlooked His outstretched hand through the care and kindness of others?

Today's Reflection

_____
_____
_____
_____
_____
_____
_____
_____
_____
_____
_____
_____
_____
_____
_____
_____
_____

Today's Prayer

_____
_____
_____
_____
_____

# Empty Bowls

The apostles left the Sanhedrin, rejoicing
because they had been counted worthy
of suffering disgrace for the Name.
—Acts 5:41

---

On Day 29, I have much more to say about my mom, but for now, let me explain a little about my mom's courage and the church family's wisdom toward us prisoners. In essence, my mom became a lifeline for us Christians.

On several occasions, especially after prison assemblies, we Christians were made to remain after all others were dismissed. The officials would ask a series of questions, trying to ascertain more information to use against us.

They persistently asked, "Who were your visitors, and what relations are they to you?"

To say they were family was a safe and verifiable answer. To say they were friends was almost certain they would be taken into custody and interrogated.

Some fast-thinking sisters realized that they were asking these questions in order to entrap our sisters and brothers in Christ who might be delivering aid to us. So since my home was nearest to the prison facility, my mom volunteered to be the go-between for the church. She would deliver cash to me to put into my prison account in order to purchase vouchers to make purchases from the prison store. Her courageous and loving hands delivered all clothing, shoes, and food items. We all rejoiced and freely shared these blessings of provision. However, harshness and cruelty often punctuated our delightful celebrations of thanksgiving.

Informants abound in prison, and they are generously rewarded for their information, especially against Christians. It was not long for guards and inmates alike to spot Christians secretly praying, worshiping, sharing, or encouraging one another as the Scripture exhorts us to do. Once we are singled out, we become targets for extraordinary harassment and abuse. The following are a few examples.

Prison guards have special assignments and departments that they are accountable to. Two such departments are work/factory guards and reeducation guards. Whenever the reeducation guards were on kitchen duty, they would single out us Christians as we came through the lunch line.

They would ask, "Do you still believe in your Jesus?"

We would answer, "Yes!"

We were then told to step out of the lunch line and stand against the wall with our empty bowls until we changed our minds.

As you might well imagine, we would not deny our Lord Jesus, especially for the unhealthy food the prison was dishing out. After the lunch hour, we were forced to go back to work hungry and to fill our daily quotas. Then would come dinnertime.

When the dinner hour would come around and we were in the dinner line, we would be asked once again, "Do you still believe in your Jesus?"

We knew what would happen if we answered in the affirmative. But it was our badge of honor to suffer for our Jesus. "Yes, Jesus is our Lord!"

"Go, stand against the wall and examine yourself!" the food service guard would exclaim. Their parting shot would be, "Till you change your mind about this Jesus."

We would sometimes be forced to stand with empty bowls in hand until one o'clock in the morning. We would then be dismissed without lunch and dinner to get a few hours of sleep, only to start the day over again.

Some of our fellow inmates were sympathetic to our plight, while others simply thought us fools. What we thought about ourselves was more important. And what Jesus thought of us was of paramount significance.

I recall other random acts of cruelty when a new sister arrived in the prison and an informant caught her praying. This new sister was dragged out of her cell and thrown out into the cold winter night as punishment. It was a miracle from God that she did not die from this abuse.

Another sister wrote notes of encouragement to be distributed among us, and an informant reported her to officials. Officials and informants plotted together to catch my sisters in the act of encouraging others. We were under 24-7 surveillance.

At prison assemblies, we Christians were singled out for verbal abuse and shame in the presence of all inmates.

After some events, we were singled out once again, made to answer questions such as:

- Who supports you? Family or friends? *(My family! This was a way to entrap us)*
- Hasn't your religion brainwashed you? *(No, my faith makes me better.)*
- Don't we treat you well? *(Not so. We are treated as the worst criminals. Unfair!)*
- Isn't your religion just another cult? *(No, Jesus is the way, truth, and life.)*

With threats and cursing, they continued to remind us of the prohibition against prayer, fellowship, and sharing the gospel. Such exclusions made us renew our commitment to Jesus. We decided that we sisters would have assigned days of fasting and prayer. Three sisters daily would have this privilege assignment, and we would rotate the honor. The three main things that we prayed about was:

- God, grant us more time for the sisters to
- Lord, protect our church family as they continued to spread the gospel, especially our elders
- Spirit, draw our fellow inmates to you as well as the guards and prison officials

What we wanted to accomplish while in prison was to build bridges and make friends with everyone. We wanted to live at peace with all people as the Scripture admonishes us. We were people of the Way (Acts 9:2; 18:25; 19:9, 23). We were disciples of the Lord Jesus Christ, following Him even to the place of disgrace.

While I was free, I could not imagine what suffering disgrace for the name would mean. But with each new wave of hostility, He made us stronger and gave us an excellent standing and great assurance in our faith in Christ Jesus.

# What Do You Think?

What opportunities has the Lord given you to share in His disgrace: at home, school, work, or among your own family? Must we have the last word, or does that belong to Jesus?

Today's Reflection

_____
_____
_____
_____
_____
_____
_____
_____
_____
_____
_____
_____
_____
_____
_____
_____

Today's Prayer

_____
_____
_____
_____

# Holidays in Lao Jiao

These people are not drunk, as you suppose.

—Acts 2:15

---

Holidays in Lao Jiao were bright moments in a dark world. We celebrated only a few holidays, but oh, what great fun they were: Harvest Moon Festival, Chinese New Year, and the occasional beating-our-deadlines-and-quotas party.

A holiday meal was prepared. (This meant that meat was sparingly distributed in the vats of vegetables.) And recreational arts were the mainstay of these celebrations. Everyone was encouraged to express herself in singing, dancing, writing, and game playing. I participated in in dancing, singing, and writing, as did most of my sisters in the Lord. By dancing, I am referring to common dancing, not part of the dance troupe.

All factory workers were brought into a large room where a sound system was set up and music began to fill the air. Songs of romance, patriotism, and life carried us away from the harsh conditions and labor in the factory.

When the music sounded, we would rush to our friends and sisters to share the joy of dancing.

Generally speaking, those inmates whose crime was drugs were really outgoing and bold, and we sisters were generally quiet and reserved. However, once the music struck and dancing began, everything changed. Our drug friends would boldly pull us out to the dance floor where the fun was being had. Though reluctant, we joined in the great entertainment.

I refer to them as my *drug friends*, but I do not mean that we approved of drugs. (We certainly do not.) But that was their offense that landed them in Lao Jiao. Our dances, whether Christian or criminal, were just clean fun and good-natured.

These dances afforded us some recreation and fun and gave us time to catch up with the well-being of the sisters. Dances were morale boosters for all and lifted our spirits, if only for the moment.

I also participated in sing-alongs, another holiday pastime. Sing-alongs were open mic events. Music would play, and inmates would line up to belt out their favorite tunes. Some would sing love songs, while others would do patriotic tunes. And still others would sing the Chinese version of the blues, crooning about the regrets of their lives.

When the beat was up-tempo, everyone would join in hand clapping. When the beat was somber, some would share in the sorrow. Throughout this sing-along, there were those who talked through every song, giving only little attention to who or what was being performed up front.

Then we sisters decided to chime in the moment by singing a worship song to the Lord. Three of us stepped up to the mic. There was no background music played, no tempo to clap to, and no lyrics that the inmates were familiar with. We three just stepped up to the front, and on my cue, we started to sing a cappella,

*We are Pilgrims of the Way*
*Our experience has brought us together*
*Sharing the same joy*
*Sharing the same suffering*
*Making us one in Spirit*
*Thank you God for bringing us here*
*We praise You;*
*Grace and salvation are Yours...*

Guards and inmates alike didn't know how to respond. They stood there in hushed silence as we lifted our voices in praise. You could hear a pin drop. When we finished the worship song, all was still and silent. Even the officials overseeing the event were stunned, and everyone applauded the performance. Fellow inmates later told us that our song was so beautiful. For me, what was so amazing was that our simple worship song captivated all their attention. And for one brief moment, like never before, a gentle wind swept through all present.

Writing was also encouraged during these celebrations. I had the privilege of writing a script for *Kuai Ban*, a comedic word game set to rhythm. It was so successful that the warden of our Lao Jiao asked me to write a special Kuai Ban to compete against the men's prison. God gave me favor in her eyes, if only for the moment.

Some of the other sisters and I wrote articles about issues of life, yet biblical principles and precepts guided our writings. When we sang our song, it was a spontaneous performance with no time for officials to censor, but in our writings, we had to be "shrewd as serpents and gentle as doves" (Matt. 10:16). It was astounding to see how well received our writings were, and many commented on the truthfulness of what we had written. The essence of our writing was "faith, hope, and love. But the greatest of these is love." 1Corinthians 13:13. Little did they know they were agreeing with God.

These holidays presented opportunities, unbeknownst to us, that would cause both officials and inmates to change their minds, albeit slowly, about Christians.

We Christians have been the butt of jokes and the scorn of the intelligent. We are considered as mentally sick, superstitious, or just plain stupid. Now, Jesus had lifted the low estate of His people before the eyes of the unbeliever. It was as though the ancient words have come around that say, "These people are not drunk, as you suppose."

# What Do You Think?

Isn't it amazing to see how God uses even small, simple events or moments to do His work through us? Will you allow yourself to step up and be used of Him in this day?

Today's Reflection

_____
_____
_____
_____
_____
_____
_____
_____
_____
_____
_____
_____
_____
_____
_____

Today's Prayer

_____
_____
_____
_____

Day 28

# The Unfailing Love of My Mom

I am reminded of your sincere faith, which first lived in your grandmother Lois and in your mother Eunice and, I am persuaded, now lives in you also.
—2 Timothy 1:15

One very hot summer day, our prison duties were to toil in the peanut fields. We worked all morning long, tending the peanut crop, and near midday, guards conducted a head count. Then we were all marched two miles back to the prison yard.

While on our way to the yard, the guard said, "Your mom is here to visit you." And she then said, "She is old. What kind of daughter are you? You should be ashamed of yourself!"

These words, though delivered brutally, had some ring of truth to them. Mom's visits were highlights for me, yet I could not help but have mixed feelings as I would head to the visiting area. I would experience sorrow over the fact that I was my mom's cross to bear and I would feel helpless to aid her in any way. In China, we are taught that children are to grow up and be a help and aid to their aging parents, and I found myself unable to help yet always receiving aid from my mom. She never complained about this, but I harbored this in my heart.

In the prison yard, to my left as we marched in were the administration offices. Straight ahead was the entry to the prison dorms, and to my right was the visitor waiting area.

Upon entry of the prison yard, I quickly glanced over to the visitor area to see if I could spot Mom. I immediately saw her white hair, and her eyes were anxiously searching the eighty women who now occupied the prison yard.

I saw her before she saw me. At that moment, my heart would sink, making my mom go through all this trouble to care for me. *Maybe the guard was on to something?* I thought privately.

"Liu, Sarah!" the officer shouted. She was confirming our presence after the march from the peanut fields.

I answered back, and I was told to go in the dorms and clean up and change my clothes.

"Your mom is waiting for you."

I did not clean up or change my clothes. I didn't go to lunch. I waited eagerly to have my name called once again to be escorted to the visitor area. Finally, my name was called, and I excitedly proceeded to the visitor area, where my elderly mom, just as eager as I was, waited for me.

In my culture, there is no overt demonstration of affection. Yet emotions were running high in both of our hearts. Our eyes tell the story.

Once settled in our visiting room with my mom, the guard, and me, her first words were, "You're skinnier and very dark!"

We both nervously glanced at the guard, who would sometimes stare at us with disapproval and would appear aloof at other times. It was hard to make out what they were thinking.

"Chicken. Have some," Mom invited.

I looked at the guard for some sign of approval and then proceeded to indulge in the best chicken dinner ever.

"Here's clothes and shoes for you," she added.

The season was about to change, and the change could be dramatic. I desperately needed these clothes. What is more, these were store-bought garments. How special she would make me feel. There was no sign of burden bearing on her part.

Then she asked, "Do you need money for prison vouchers? I have money for you. Take it."

I glanced again at the guard and accepted the money.

During that visit, she said, "I am your mom, but the Lord made me the mom of all the other sisters in prison with you." And as she parted, she said, "Share these provisions I brought for you."

I should have expected this from her, but I had such exclusive feelings for my mom that such an idea took me aback. It was true. She loved us all. And I had to learn to share this incredibly bighearted woman with everyone else.

"You have five more minutes," the guard informed us.

I thought, *How quickly our thirty minutes pass.*

The moment of our good-bye had come. The guard ordered me to stand and exit the visiting room first. My mom and I both stood, and I was escorted out. I could feel my mom watching my every move.

Once the barred door closed, I turned to watch my dear mom exit the room. She turned, and I could see her form walk through the door. I had the deepest sense and most profound gratitude for such a mom as this. Her steadfastness in the Lord and her service to the saints was amazing. What a beautiful sincere faith she had. *Lord, make me like that too*, I thought.

# What Do You Think?

Who has played the significant role of handing down a sincere faith to you? To whom will you pass it on to? Why not pray for him or her this day?

Today's Reflection

_____

_____

_____

_____

_____

_____

_____

_____

_____

_____

_____

_____

_____

_____

_____

_____

Today's Prayer

_____

_____

_____

_____

Day 29

# Not in My Wildest Imagination

As the heavens are higher than the earth,
so are my ways higher than your ways
and my thoughts than your thoughts.

—Isaiah 55:9

---

It was nine o'clock on a cold winter's night when I heard my name shouted out, "Liu, Sarah," along with three other sisters' names. We were being called to go to the administration office. *What's going on?* I thought.

I knew of no reason that I should be called on. I did notice that the Christians were called upon.

Since I had become a seasoned prisoner, it raised no alarm when my name was called out. However, to have a group of Christians called at the same time is a cause for apprehension. *Why all of us? What are we being accused of?* I initially thought.

When we arrived in the administration area, the officer in charge of the prison release program met us and invited us into her office. We all looked at one another, sharing the same thoughts and concerns.

When we had taken our seats, the officers told us, "Tomorrow, all four of you will be released."

In stunning surprise, I thought, *All four to be released?*

Up to this point, I had convinced myself that, of all incarcerated Christians, I would be the last one released. Now with these words still ringing in my ears, I wanted to shout for joy, but we had been conditioned not to show any emotion, lest we show our heart to others, and those others would use it against us.

The officer further stated, "You will be released tomorrow morning."

*What? Less than one day to prepare for our departure?* I thought. Then upon second reflection, I thought, *I'll take it.*

On the one hand, we rejoiced afterward to know that we were all being released together and we were the last four Christians in that institution and no one would be left behind. Then on the other hand, we were angry that they had given us such a short notice. The other three sisters had no one they could call because their hometowns were a great distance away. Even if they were notified, it would have taken some families at least a week to come and retrieve their loved ones.

The three sisters looked to me because my hometown was not far. "Someone could come retrieve the four of us and take us to your hometown," they discussed.

My inner struggle was that I knew I would not return to my hometown. I would go back to my church family to carry on the ministry. I turned to them and said, "I will go back to the church and not to my home." I waited to hear their response and much to my delight they responded with, "We will return with you." What relief and joy in knowing what our next step was.

"But who will collect us?" their faces expressed.

Early the next morning, we hurried to get our belongings together. We were called to the administration offices once again to be processed for release and given one more admonition.

"We know you haven't changed," she growled at us. "If you keep believing in Jesus, you will land back here in Lao Jiao!" Those were her last words to us.

We were escorted to the main gate and released. After a quick discussion, we decided to walk to the main highway, and perhaps the Lord would give us some direction.

As we reached the highway, we couldn't believe our eyes.

"Look! It's Sister Lanlan!" one of the sisters shouted.

Sister Lanlan was a member of our church, and she was somehow alerted that we were being released. So she waited for us at a distance with her three-wheeled motor car. What a sight for sore eyes!

She hurried us in the car, lest police officers lying in wait would arrest us again. Once on the road, Sister Lanlan said "Sister Li, who was released before you, told me that you too were about to be released. When I saw all four of you on the road, I was overjoyed and hurried to pick you up. Now we are together again."

"How long had you waited for us?" I asked.

"For many days, patiently waiting on this road for your discharge" was her reply.

"We didn't even know we were being released," I said to her.

Somehow or other, the church ascertained our release and had prepared to collect us. Thank God for a patient and faithful sister!

That day, we were taken to Wuhan, where our host family kindly received us. That night, the host family laid out a fantastic dinner. It was beautiful, plentiful, and delicious. I thought, *How Lao Jiao has numbed me to the simple pleasure of this life.* Now amongst friends, I was dining on real food with genuine meat and good drink. I was laughing and talking freely among people I love.

During our one-month stay in Wuhan, we met up with other sisters and brothers who had been released from the various prisons. What a reunion that was, recounting our sundry experiences in prison, people we met, situations the Lord delivered us from, and the suffering we all endured. As you can imagine, there was laughter, serious discussion, and tears, some of sorrow and others of joy.

How good it was to read the Bible, pray, worship, and pray some more. We all needed time to heal both spiritually and physically. I'm not sure anyone went back to life as it once was. I know I didn't.

Teacher Bob Fu of China Aid contacted us and asked us to record our experiences so the outside world could know our stories. We recounted in writing the works of God and the deeds of men and government. We were happy to give testimony to what was happening to us Christians. What gave us a greater impetus to write these reports was that, by outside world, we understood to mean primarily the United States. And it was reported to us that the president of this outside world was a Christian! So our church fervently prayed for George W. Bush and the outside world. This gave us hope that maybe the outside world could help China become good.

After our rest and recuperation was completed, we all went back out to our respective fields of ministry. Because of the government's crackdown on our church, all of us had to assume a wider scope to the ministry. Resources were running scarce, and the crackdown kept us on the edge of our faith. But through all this, Jesus demonstrated His faithfulness and love like the Good Shepherd He is.

While ministering the Word in Sichuan, at our autumn mountain retreat, near the end of the third week, one sister reported that we had missed an important phone call from Hubei. Since phone reception in our area was really bad, we had to travel to a better location. We finally were able to return the call.

"Hello, this is Sarah," I said to the person on the other end. "I'm returning your phone call."

The voice was a man's, and I immediately and without introduction knew who it was. This was one of our main church leaders, Brother Zhen Li. My first thought after recognizing his voice was that he would be the bearer of bad news, such as the crackdown had widened and we needed to flee for our lives or that someone was hurt or in trouble. I didn't normally get calls from our leaders.

"You need to come back quickly," he said in a hurried tone.

"For what?" I asked.

"We cannot speak by phone. Too important. Come back quickly!" he urgently requested.

I reminded Brother Li that I still had one week of Bible school and I was one of two main speakers.

Brother Li then responded, "Come back as soon as possible."

"I will," I assured him.

In Hubei, I met with Brother Li and several other leaders. As I looked around the room, I wondered what all this might mean. *How did I figure in their plans?* I thought.

"Okay, let's pray," said Brother Li.

Now I knew it was serious and important.

"Sister Sarah," Brother Li continued, "we have been in contact with Teacher Bob Fu of China Aid, and he has asked us to send him one eyewitness to what is happening to us here in China. We leaders prayed about whom to send to Teacher Fu and decided it would be you."

I heard the words, and I think I understand their meaning, but it all seemed surreal in that moment. Three threads of thought instantly ran through my mind:

1. How can this be since the crackdown has grown increasingly fierce? Many homes were demolished where we conducted Bible studies and prayer. Many sisters and brothers have been arrested and tortured

for the faith. Many of our families have been torn apart, having to make heart-wrenching decisions. And now I'm supposed to leave?

2. If this, what they say, would come to pass, my life would take a quantum leap to the outside world. I am at home in a small setting with Bible studies, prayer meetings, and evangelism in local villages. But the outside world? "Lord, this knowledge is too great for me. It is more than I can bear," I cried.

3. Surely there were more qualified people than I was. Who am I that I should have this task bestowed upon me?

How right was the great prophet Isaiah when he spoke the very words of God and said, "As the heavens are higher than the earth, so are my ways higher than your ways and my thoughts than your thoughts"? Isaiah 55:9.

# What Do You Think?

Has the Lord ever taken you to a place, a situation that you felt inadequate to be in? What was your response, or what should your response be?

Today's Reflection

_____

_____

_____

_____

_____

_____

_____

_____

_____

_____

_____

_____

_____

_____

_____

_____

Today's Prayer

_____

_____

_____

_____

# The First Step on a Long Journey

Where can I go from your Spirit? Where can I flee from your presence? If I go up to the heavens, you are there; if I make my bed in the depths, you are there. If I rise on the wings of the dawn, if I settle on the far side of the sea, even there your hand will guide me, your right hand will hold me fast.

—Psalm 139:7–10

———————

The night before, there was a gathering of church leaders. Brother Zheng Li and several of the other leaders gathered for a meal of spicy lamb hot pot. But instead of the talk and laughter that would usually accompany such an occasion, it was quiet and somber. It was muted because I was not the church's first attempt to get someone out of China to tell our story. Previous attempts were made, and all failed. We were all so uncertain as to the outcome of this attempt.

Teacher Bob Fu intentionally gave us no details about the escape route or modes of transportation. To us, it was all guesswork. It was on a need-to-know basis.

I asked aloud, "How long will the trip take?"

They assured me, "No more than a month at sea."

*A month?!* thought I.

Up to this point, the longest boat trip I had taken was across the Yangtze River, which only takes four hours. But the truth was that none of us had a clue. In a way, the sisters and brothers that night were trying to calm my fears. The Lord bless them for their love and concern!

"The testimonies ... don't forget the testimonies!" I was reminded.

The most important reason for the trip was the handwritten testimonies from our church sisters and brothers concerning the government's abuse and their walk with God in the midst of injustice.

One of my sisters told me, "You will be meeting very important people. You must look important too," she admonished.

Because of this, the church purchased two outfits for me: one for traveling and one for meeting important people.

The sisters explained, "Your important clothes should be a dark color and such and such style." Finally after shopping and finding these important clothes, they said, "You have what you need!"

A point of humor was that we all believed that whatever the weather conditions and season was for us in China, it existed for the rest of the world as well. And that included America. Since I was leaving in the deep of winter, I was prepared for winter anywhere on the globe!

Brother Li told me, "You can't forget the gift for Teacher Bob Fu."

"What is that?" I asked.

"Ah, it's a very special gift that I think Teacher Fu will love," he asserted confidently.

"Yes, but what gift is that?" I responded.

And in grand fashion, Brother Li announced, "A Wuchang fish!"

"A Wuchang fish!" I replied.

"Yes, that is a popular fish for taste and medicinal reasons."

With testimonies, new clothes to meet important people, and a Wuchang fish, I was ready to begin my month long voyage to America.

We gave ourselves to prayer one last time. Then it was off to the train station. We flagged down a couple of taxis to take all seven of us: four sisters, two brothers, and me. We kept our conversation to a minimum for fear of saying too much in the presence of the taxi drivers. One never knows who is an informant.

We were dropped off on the far side of the train station, where we had to cross a large open square. As we all crossed the square, the night was cold, and we were all bundled up. The sounds of our footsteps echoed in the square. At that moment, we all experienced a torrent of emotions. We had all been through so much together—suffered, prayed, cried, laughed, and feared amongst one another. That was all ending. Life was changing for all of us.

And this moment came down around our heads. Words could not express what each of us felt. We all just knew. We all said our good-byes, and with tears in our eyes, I and the two sisters who were assigned to travel with me turned and entered the train. Our friends stayed on the platform, and we pulled away until I could see them no more.

Arriving at our destination, we waited for our next set of instructions. The mobile phone rang.

"Hello ... Yes, this is Sister Aimu."

We all gathered around the phone, straining to listen to the conversation. As you can imagine, it was all inaudible to us. We just heard, "dui ... dui ... dui (yes ... yes ... yes)."

"What did Teacher Fu say?" we eagerly inquired.

"He said we were to meet a sister tomorrow and we are to give you over to her," Aimu answered.

We made contact the next day with this sister. My two companions took me to a prearranged location for a rendezvous. When we arrived, all of us kept our distance from one another. The handoff sister led the way. I followed. Then my two companions came after me. All stayed at a distance so as to appear as strangers to each other and not to draw attention to ourselves.

As we traveled the narrow, dusty path near the border's edge, we rounded a corner. As I was about to lose sight of my traveling companion, I looked back as we all frantically waved good-bye one last time. Then they were out of sight.

As my sister was leading me down the path, I knew we were close to the border. Out of nowhere, two men appeared and became our new guides. I later found out that they were locals entrusted with getting us near the border's edge.

As we rounded the last curve of our trek on this side of China, our two guides vanished from the sight of the sister and me. Then a pastor and his two assistants were waiting for us with a minivan, ready to take us to the last border crossing.

We were rushed into the van, and I was immediately hidden beneath one of the back row seats and covered with blankets and other traveling items. From this moment on, I was literally in the dark. All five of us were traversing this rough path while heading to the border station. We stopped. The engine was turned off. My new traveling companions opened the doors, and I heard footsteps leading away from the van. Then all was quiet. I do not know how long they were gone, but it felt like a lifetime.

"Hide me like the two spies in Jericho," I prayed. "Even this remote place is not hidden from You," I silently cried.

Then I heard the sound of footsteps approaching the van. Doors opened, passengers climbed in, the engine started, and off we went. *Are we over the border?* I wondered.

I was comforted when I heard their voices. They were not excited, which was a good sign, and spoke in normal conversational tones in American English.

I concluded that we were across the border. *We've crossed the border*, I thought. *Thank You, Jesus!*

We drove for another half hour. We stopped, and the engine was turned off. The doors were opened, and the blankets were removed...

# What Do You Think?

So often, we want to know and control outcomes. Could it be that the only path for doing His will is to trust?

Today's Reflection

_____
_____
_____
_____
_____
_____
_____
_____
_____
_____
_____
_____
_____
_____
_____
_____
_____

Today's Prayer

_____
_____
_____
_____